An Esoteric Reading of Biblical Symbolism

AN ESOTERIC READING OF
BIBLICAL SYMBOLISM

AN ESOTERIC READING OF BIBLICAL SYMBOLISM

BY

HARRIET TUTTLE BARTLETT

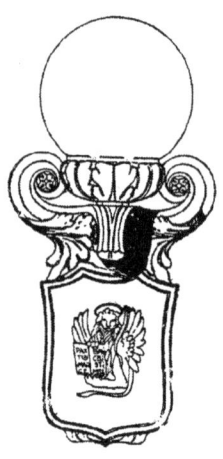

SAN FRANCISCO
PHILOPOLIS PRESS
1916

COPYRIGHT 1916
BY
HARRIET TUTTLE BARTLETT

TABLE OF CONTENTS.

		Page
Foreword		1
Introduction		3
Plate		7
Explanation of Plate		8
Chapter I.	Keynote of the Bible	11
Chapter II.	Mysteries	15
Chapter III.	Metaphysical Ideas of the Ancient Hebrews	29
Chapter IV.	The Story of Creation	38
Chapter V.	Significance of the Genealogy of Shem and the Work of Abraham and Lot	46
Chapter VI.	Noah and the Flood	53
Chapter VII.	The Significance of the Two Covenants of Abraham	62
Chapter VIII.	Moses	67
Chapter IX.	Reincarnation in the Bible	77
Chapter X.	Can Jesus Be Identified In Other Lives?	82
Chapter XI.	Are These Some Incarnations of Our Blessed Christ?	92
Chapter XII.	The Visions of Ezekiel	139
Chapter XIII.	Jehovah Commanded no Bloody Sacrifices	151
Chapter XIV.	Light Thrown on Obscure Passages	157
Glossary of Symbols and Obsolete Words		161

FOREWORD.

I send this little book out into the world as an humble tribute to the cause of truth, with heartfelt gratitude to the Master Jesus for the patient guidance and illuminations that have been given me during the years that I have been pondering over the pages of the Scriptures of the Aryan race, realizing fully that I have sensed but a very small part of the wonders that lie hidden beneath the wonderful symbolic utterances of that marvelous Mystic Book, but full of joy that I have found enough to reveal to me something of the wondrous beauty of God's plan for the evolution of man.

Mistakes, there are many, no doubt, that better scholarship, or greater spiritual perceptions may reveal, as time goes on, but I have tried to give it exactly as it was presented to my mind, and what mistakes there are, are the result of undeveloped faculties trying to grasp ideas too great for them to comprehend. These facts, however, came to me with such illuminative force, that I cannot but hope that they may prove equally helpful to others who are struggling in the bonds of mistaken conceptions of what the Bible really teaches.

We are standing upon but the threshold of the Temple of Truth, and can but glimpse the glories lying within, but each step we take forward brings us nearer to the vision celestial; and no effort made with the right motive will be lost. "Knowing this first, that no prophecy of Scripture is of special interpretation. For no prophecy ever came by the will of man: but man spake from God being moved by the Holy Spirit." II Peter, 1, 20 and 21. Here we are justified in searching out the hidden inner meaning, as, indeed, we are in many passages that refer to the "Mysteries of Jesus."

Occultists tell us that all Scripture has seven different meanings intended to assist man at each of the seven different planes of his evolution, and this seems to be true. At each step that we take, we find that the tale told is just what we most need to direct us along the path. To the writer they have ever spoken in no uncertain tone.

These illuminations have brought to me such unspeakable joy, and peace, such conviction and strength of inspiration, that to those at the same stage of progress I feel sure that they must of necessity come as a blessing. To those farther along upon the path, they will perhaps seem crude, while to those not so far advanced they may in some cases be unintelligible. They are sent out to those who need them, to those to whom they appeal. May the Master bless them as they start upon their long journey to hunt the hearts that need them; may they in some small way, help to make straight the way of the Great Master Christ, when He again comes to this sin-sick old world; and may they help, at least a few earnest souls to gain the token by which they may know Him when He appears.

HARRIET TUTTLE BARTLETT.

INTRODUCTION.

It may be well to explain in a few words, something of the method by which these conclusions have been arrived at.

The Bible read in the literal way that is customary with the purely orthodox, fails to stand the test of historic and scientific research, because of the erroneous assumptions of the translators, who were misled by lack of the information that is now coming in such abundance to us. It is gratifying to see that the recent translators have discarded the foolish chronology which has caused so much trouble, and while it is somewhat disconcerting to think of the many reckonings that are thrown into confusion as to time by this step, yet it was positively necessary to understand things as they are.

Scientific investigation has done much in giving us data upon which to calculate, in a general way, but to Oriental research, especially through philological lines, do we owe much of the information that is proving a golden key by which we may unlock the storehouses of ancient wisdom that throw light upon the obscure portions of our Sacred Book. To state it briefly, these investigations have brought out the fact that the most ancient Sacred MSS. gave out the same great fundamental truths upon which our own religion is based. Many great natural laws are explained and about the same ethical standard is upheld as we have been accustomed to connect with the teachings of our own faith; the difference being, if any, rather in favor of the superiority of the standard upheld by the ancients as being attainable. "Be ye therefore perfect even as your Father in heaven is perfect" was to them an attainable ideal, while to us it seems a monstrous assumption.

As we study, we see that the weakness in our own system lies in the fact that the Christian Mysteries have been temporarily lost, due to the political aspirations of the church from the fourth century, but abundant evidence exists that they were a part of the Apostolic Church, and that the early Church Fathers owed their unusual spiritual strength to the influence of this special training.

We find there are certain symbols that are universal, to which the hidden truths have been confided during the ages, and that these symbols tell the same tale, no matter where they may be found, no matter what the language of the people may be. Then we look and find these same symbols telling the same story in our own Bible. The Hebrew language lent itself with unusual felicity to the veiled work of the Mysteries, as it was a purely consonantal language, each letter having a numerical value, and each number having an esoteric significance. It is not surprising that the message has remained hidden under the circumstances. It was perfectly safe until the time was ripe for its disclosure. Evidently the Master's will controlled the situation. Not until man's intuition develops will the secrets of the ages be revealed to him.

The translation of the personal nouns and geographical names, often gives the key to an allegory, but, in this line of work, one is often hindered by the fact that the meaning of the word has been lost in the course of the ages. By taking the root, however, tracing it back as nearly as possible to its mother tongue, one may often get a meaning that clearly dovetails with the obvious meaning of the text in such a way as to justify the inference that the right one has been found, or at least something very near to it.

In studying the allegorical meaning of the Bible the writer finds that it is wise to stick to the spiritual meaning consistently all the way through, not read one passage allegorically and the next literally which causes the garbled result so often obtained by Biblical scholars.

This line of study, however, demonstrates that the lower mind alone cannot give satisfactory results. To the intuition must we turn if the higher truths are to become ours. For that reason Scripture should always be studied in a prayerful spirit. Personally, the writer has always called directly upon the Master Jesus for guidance, and all that has been given at such times, when the flash of illumination has been accompanied by a sense of "The Presence" has withstood the test of the most careful investigation that she has been able to make from information available. The first glimpse has not always been complete, and

INTRODUCTION

additional information given later has made the matter clearer, but she has never yet been obliged to admit one of these glimpses of truth to be erroneous; invariably they have proven true, though perhaps in a much larger way than was at first perceived. Gradually she has learned that in the consciousness of at-one-ment of Spirit it is but necessary to touch the hem of His Spiritual garments, or His Spiritual vibrations, that virtue may flow from Him. He says, "Behold, I stand at the door and knock, if any man open the door I will come in unto him, and will sup with him, and he with Me."

"Remember that everyone who meditates upon the Master makes a definite link with him which shows to clairvoyant vision as a kind of line of light. The Master always subconsciously feels the impinging of such a line, and sends out along it in response a steady stream of magnetism which continues to play long after the meditation is over. The regular practice of such meditation and concentration is of the utmost help to the aspirant, and the regularity is one of the most important factors in producing results." Vol. I, "Inner Life," by C. W. Leadbeater, page 34.

This experience is one that has often been found in Christian Mystics, it has not originated with the writer, but the influx of Oriental Information has rendered what has been received much more intelligible than it would otherwise have been.

The writer makes no pretense of being able to read the akasic records, and in some instances may have taken what was meant for merely a type for a real incarnation of a Great One, but such matters will be straightened out by more expert investigators, and need not detract from the value of the truths revealed Errors there must be, of course, in a work bringing out ideas so new to the mind trained in the orthodox school, and dealing with things so far transcending what that mind is accustomed to handling; but to the spiritually minded these pages may open up an unexplored mine of riches, and they may get far more than the writer has, having better trained inner perceptions that will need but the hint to make them able to penetrate to the Inner Sanctuary, To the materialistic mind there will be nothing to appeal in this book. Spiritual truths may be apprehended by Spirit alone.

The writer has found that of necessity there must be more

repetitions in a work like this, than is considered permissible in good composition. The newness of the ideas makes it necessary to connect the mind with what has gone before to make each stage clear. So far as possible she has tried to avoid this. However, she realizes that there are still far too many such cases to suit good taste but can see no way to avoid it if the points are made clear without too great a demand upon the reader's memory.

INVOLUTION AND EVOLUTION OF THE SPIRIT OF MAN.

I	Father	⊖	1st Logos	543
H	Son	⊖	2nd "	
VH	Holy Spirit	⊕	3rd "	HVA
I.	Yod.	Masc.	Will	
H.	Hevah.	fem.	Wisdom	
VH.		Creative Activity		
		Understanding.		
Nirvana		7 Sephiroth		
		7 Angels Before Throne		
		7 Logoi		
Archetypal		Ego	Messiah	
		⊙	✡ 888	
Man			Buddhic Plane	
Mental		Adam	Soul ○	
			or	
Dust Land		Dust	Causal Body	
Astral			Emotional	
Man { Adam / Eve }		◎	Desire Plane	
Sand Land			IHT-Jesus-318	
Black Land			Cain } Mäia	
Cush-Egypt		◎	Abel } Mss }	
Wilderness			Moses 345 }	
Great Battle Of Spirit and Matter				

HARRIET TUTTLE BARTLETT

EXPLANATION OF PLATE.

The Great V shows Spirit descending into matter until it becomes immeshed in bodies of each of the planes, then it turns its face toward the Father again, and by conquering the planes one by one mounts on its way back to the Father from whom it came.

The horizontal lines divide the planes but simply for the sake of clearness in study. The matter really interpenetrates and the matter of all planes is to be found in any given spot at any time. These planes simply refer to matter in different degrees of density.

On the highest plane we have the Three Great Outpourings of the Solar Logos (God) as they are directed toward the seven planes directly concerning us. There are still higher and higher Great Ones, but the Bible does not dwell upon that except to recognize the Hierarchies in a general way.

Yod, I, is a masculine potency and is the Will aspect of the Logos.

H, Hevah, translated Eve, is the Love Wisdom aspect of the creative form producing power of the Universe, spoken of by the Christian as the "Son."

V H, We He, is the great creative activity of the Logos spoken of by the Christian as the Holy Spirit. This outpouring brought into being the perfected atom of each plane making possible the form producing work.

The seven Sephiroth are the seven attributes of God, or the seven great creative Agents of the Logos manifesting those attributes. The seven Planetary Logoi.

The Archetypal Man lies upon the Buddhic or Christ Plane and the evolving man rises to that plane when he conquers matter and becomes the Master of Compassion.

On this Buddhic Plane the descending Ego lay till provided with a body by Lord Jehovah, who gave him a mental body.

EXPLANATION OF PLATE

The symbolism makes the Mental Plane the Dust Land, and Adam was given a body of dust, so he is the Dust Adam of H. P. B.

On the Astral, or Emotional and Desire Plane, the Sand Land of the allegory, we find H. P. B.'s "Shadow Adam." Matter has become so dense that it hampers the Spirit and its vibration begin to control. "The Woman" (body) "Thou gavest me she did it."

The Physical Plane is the Black Land, the Land of Cush, Egypt, the Wilderness of Ignorance. Here is fought the great battle of Spirit and matter. At last the day comes when the Spirit turns its face toward the Father who sent it out, and then begins to mount by conquering each plane.

Moses is symbol of the perfected Physical as well as the great Manu of the fifth root race. His number is 345, the number of God's back.

543 is the number of God's face.

543 plus 345 makes 888, the number of the Christ. Perfect Man and perfect God make the Christ Man.

The Soul or Causal Body is built by man's efforts to get back to God, and can be lost, but the Spirit must return to God who sent it out.

I H T, the symbol of Jesus, may be read God the Father and God the Son working on the Desire Plane. 318, his number, means purity.

M S S, symbol of Moses, may be read Matter with double amount of Wisdom.

Mäia means Matter or Mother.

CHAPTER I.

THE KEY NOTE OF THE BIBLE.

What is the key note of the Bible? Is it possible to find a key note in these sixty-five books that we call our Bible? These books supposed to be written by all sorts and conditions of men, during many different periods in the world's history, written by men who, in many instances, could have no way of knowing anything about their predecessors, nor could they have foreseen the destiny of their work, unless they were unusually gifted seers; can it be possible that there is a unifying chord running through such a tangled mass of strings, as many have considered these stories to be? To the writer there is a chord that sounds clear and true from cover to cover of the "Dear Old Book." If summed up in one word, perhaps no word can be used, that will so aptly convey the idea, as the simple word "Christ," if by the word Christ we mean man made God.

In the first chapter of Genesis we see the perfect thought form of Elohim manifesting. They are the architypes, or patterns, of the seven great kingdoms of nature, as they will ultimately become in the long course of evolution.

In the second chapter, beginning with the fourth verse, we see the Lord Jehovah beginning his work of starting the great evolutionary march by which these kingdoms are to gain perfection, which is the destiny shown to be theirs upon the higher planes. The egos of humanity have already advanced up to the human stage upon another chain of planets, and are now lying upon the Buddhic Plane ready for their start upon this earth. Lord Jehovah forms for them bodies of mental matter, and breathes into them the breath of life and they become "Living Souls," not Physical bodies. By desire they bring themselves down upon the Astral Plane, and the Lord Jehovah gives them an astral body to help them manifest there. Then as they gratify desire they drop into Physical bodies that are waiting for them, having evolved up from the lower kingdoms. Lord Jehovah then wraps about them the skins of animals, or their own physical skins. All is in the plural, and is the story of the descent of Spirit into matter in order to manifest.

In the experiences of the Hebrews, we see the typical stages by which man must mount on his way back to the God from whom he came. In their struggles against the bondage of Egypt (bondage of the lower nature) through the wilderness of ignorance, they slowly learn the law by experience, and from the teachings of the great Moses (Lord Jehovah) they learn that the gratification of the desires brings only disgust. At the same time they develop intellect, and at last they find themselves upon the bank of the Jordan or the descending flood of their own degenerative tendencies. Here it is that Moses lays his hands upon the shoulders of Joshua (Jesus) and that compassionate brother takes charge of the race to teach them that by purification alone can they attain the higher planes of consciousness that it is their destiny to reach. Jesus seems to be used as a type of the Masters, many of whom are shown as remaining with us and sharing in this great work for humanity. Here and there sporadic instances occur, where we see one of the people transcending the natural development of the race, and to these we see the great Initiations given, and the Initiate at once enters the work of helping the Great Ones in their effort to teach and assist humanity. In fact the whole of the book that we call Bible is the story of the typical stages in the life of humanity, not anywhere is personality accentuated. 'Tis all the story of you and of me, in the day that we attain the place that these experiences naturally develop. It is the story of the fall of spirit into matter, and its struggle to get back to God. The story of your life and my life, just as truly as it is the story of the lives of the Great Ones who preceded us upon the path.

All of the stories are in a sense historical, but when they happened is not at present revealed to us. They are used to convey a spiritual truth that is greater than any mere historic occurrence could possibly be. The Great Initiations of the Great Ones who have been the guides of humanity during the ages, are clearly shown, and the trials and victories by which they attained their present height. We are given the view of the Great Brother, whom the Jews called Lord Jehovah, guiding the race upon the physical plane; Joshua (Jesus) and the other Masters with Him, teaching them to purify themselves, and the Great Christ teaching them how to attain the "Glory I had with the Father before the world was." How to become the perfect, the God-Man.

The four letters IHVH translated Jehovah indicating the Trinity of manifestations of the Supreme is used in three senses in the Old Testament. El Jehovah, El Shadai (God Almighty) refers to the higher Trinity; while the Lord Jehovah refers to the great loving brother whom the Hindoo calls the Manu; and the "Jehovah of Hosts," or the "Lord God of Hosts," refers to the God in the heart of every man. "The light that lighteth every man that cometh into the world" (John 1). This latter is what we have been taught to call the Soul, but this is inaccurate, for the Soul is the body of the Spirit, and this inner Jehovah is the Spirit, making of ourselves the body, Soul, and Spirit, of St. Paul. This "Jehovah of Hosts," or "Lord God of Hosts," the God in the heart, is the one that is always so rebelliously chiding the race in the places that have been erroneously translated "cursed." This is the God who is jealous. He wants to rule instead of the personality. This is the struggle of the Spirit with flesh, and its cry ever is, "The Soul that sinneth it shall die." It is our higher selves struggling with our lower selves, to reduce the personality to obedience to Spirit. No curse from the "ALL WISE," no curse from the Great Loving Elder Brother "Lord Jehovah," only our higher selves chiding our lower selves because we do not please ourselves.

So there is One God. "In Him we live, and move, and have our being." There are three Great Elder Brothers (who are types of many others who have attained now), Lord Jehovah, Jesus, and Christ, and we too are the sons of the Living God making the completed Trinity. Thus does "Jehovah of Hosts" of the Old Testament become the "Christ in the heart" in the New Testament, or the new dispensation, when the race shall have attained the divine destiny so gloriously shown us by our Great Elder Brother, the first born among many brethren to attain the Goal, "Our Bright and Morning Star."

AN ESOTERIC READING OF BIBLICAL SYMBOLISM

Surely Christ is the key note of the Bible. Not Christ the Jewish man only, whom we all love to honor and whom we all know to be the great teacher of Gods and of Men, but the Great Universal Christ, Humanity, that great Son of God who shall return from the far country, and be to the Father a Son worthy to reign with Him, when He shall have attained to "the fullness of the stature of the Christ." May the magnitude of the conception fill the minds and hearts of all who read, and may they strive to emulate Him who stands with hands outspread in blessing as His glorified body is revealed to John in Revelations.

CHAPTER II.

THE MYSTERIES.

To the average reader the thought of the Mysteries has been associated with some kind of a heathen religion that flourished in ancient days. Not many have taken time even to read the article in the "Encyclopædia Britannica", much less to study the subject at length. This is largely because western ideas have been unduly distorted by lack of accurate information in regard to Oriental manners, customs, history, and ideals. We have occupied the unique position of accepting for our spiritual guidance a purely oriental book, full of the quaint imagery and beautiful figures of speech of a very poetic people, but have utterly scorned all things else Oriental, absolutely refusing to recognize the inhabitants of those countries as really civilized, dubbing them heathen, and assuming an air of great superiority over them. We have taken their book but have utterly ignored their ideas as to how it should be read, and have persisted in reading all those exquisite figures of speech as literal historic facts. Truly it is a strong argument for the inspiration of the book, that we have not gotten into more trouble than we have. Being inspired, however, and intended to guide man at every stage of his development, it has given us nourishing food for our spiritual natures in spite of all of our clumsy attempts to distort the real meaning of the passages.

The natural result of such a course of action, however, has been to cut us off from much information that might have been ours. It has closed Oriental libraries against our scholars, and has hindered their getting the instruction needed to study intelligently the great truths they found; it has prevented their penetrating to the secret archives of the wisdom of the east, through causing them to scorn the necessary preparation; and it has given to the traveler the patronizing air which has been resented, and from which he has, all unconsciously, suffered, not getting the information that otherwise would have been handed him gladly. In all these and many other ways have we suffered, simply because of our own intolerance and conceit.

Such intolerance has no justification today in the light of the flood of information that is now coming to our country, in regard to such matters. To hold to the old conservative ideas that have been so long regarded orthodox, one must close both eyes and ears, and utterly refuse the evidence of the senses. It would be a foolish waste of space and time for the writer to quote the long list of authorities that she has studied during the last thirty years, that have each contributed something to the light that has been shed upon her studies, but to get much information in little space I know of no more satisfactory works than those of Mrs. Annie Besant, and her co-worker Mr. C. L. Leadbeater, Mr. A. P. Sinnett, and Mr. G. R. S. Mead. These books bring a large amount of information into small readable volumes that are very convenient for the busy person.

However, from the article in the "Encyclopædia Britannica" upon Mysteries may be gleaned many suggestive facts. Of necessity it deals almost exclusively with the Greek Eleusinian Semi-Mysteries, in the days of their degeneration; still, in spite of this fact, many little testimonies of the original excellence of the teachings of the ancient mysteries crop out here and there, as, for instance, "The saving and healthy effect of the Eleusinian Mysteries are believed in not only by the mass of the people but by many of the most thoughtful and educated intellects, Pindar, Sophocles, Isocrates, Plutarch, etc. Plato, who finds no language too strong to stigmatize the demoralizing effect of the Orphic Mysteries (then degenerate echoes of a once pure teaching), speaks of the Eleusinian Mysteries with great respect. He compares the contemplation of 'ideas' by disembodied souls to the contemplation of the 'phasmata' revealed in the Mysteries. This saving power is expressly connected with future life; he that has been initiated has learned what will ensure his happiness hereafter. The words of Pindar, Sophocles, Isocrates agree with the words of the Homeric Hymn, that the initiated have peculiar advantages in the future world, and many other passages are equally clear and distinct." "These quotations prove a general belief that the aim of the Eleusinian Mysteries was high, and that a lasting effect was produced upon the initiated by them. This implies a high stage of religious thought such as no other ancient faith, except that of the Hebrews, attained; but a passage in a Rhodian inscription of the fifth century B. C. shows that this idea was not wholly unfamiliar in the Greek religion The first and most important condition required of those who entered the Temple at Lindus is, that they be *pure in heart,* and not conscious of any crime; conditions of ceremonial purity are enumerated as those of secondary importance."—E. B., pg. 127, Vol. M.

We must remember that the things written as to the ritual of the Mysteries are only such things as were given out to the public, not the true Mysteries, for the greater Mysteries have never been written, but are matters of the extension of the consciousness of the individual. The lessons learned bear fruit in the life lived, but are not transmitted by writing. The teaching has ever been secret, and is transmitted from mouth to ear. As Moses taught Joshua the "spoken law" he received upon the Mount, who in turn taught it to the forty receivers, who were to instruct the initiates orally; so was it in every age, so is it now, so must it ever be, if the child man is to be protected from the danger that comes from defiling things that are holy before he is able to understand the significance of his acts.

Philo Judaeus, in speaking of the Essenes says: "But the Therapeutic sect of mankind, being continually taught to see without interruption" (they functioned upon higher planes), "may well aim at obtaining a sight of the living God, and may pass by the sun" (the symbol of divinity), "which is visible to the outward sense, and never leave this order which conducts to perfect happiness. But they apply themselves to this kind of worship not because they are influenced to do so by custom, nor by advice or recommendation of any particular persons, but because they are carried away by a certain Heavenly Love." Then he goes on at length to show how they gave away their earthly possessions, caring nothing for anything that will interfere with the teaching they get in these communities where they have a plain room, no luxuries, and live most abstemiously.

He goes on to say: "And in every house there is a sacred shrine which is called the Holy Place, and the Monastery in which they retire by themselves and perform all the mysteries of a holy life."

"Therefore they always retain an imperishable recollection of God, so that, not even in their dreams, is any other subject presented to their eyes except the beauty of divine virtues, and divine powers. They also have writings of ancient men, who having been founders of one sect or another, have left behind them many memorials of an allegorical system of writing and explanations whom they take as a kind of model, and imitate the general fashion of their sect, so that they do not occupy themselves solely with contemplation."

Women also belonged to these orders, living by themselves and never mingling with the men, but getting the same teachings by assembling on the other side of a high wall where they could hear the voice of the speaker without being seen by men. We can but outline the idea in a work of this kind, and it is unnecessary to reprint what is already put out in better shape than the writer could hope to be able to do it, by Mrs. Annie Besant in her "Esoteric Christianity." No student of the Bible, no matter what his denomination may be, can afford to do without that book.

The general method of the ancient religions seems to have been to provide a simple ritualistic service for public use, such as would gradually train man to live a moral life, and develop public and private virtues, much as the Catholic Church handles her people today. After that, when the more serious minded advanced to the place where they desired more exalted knowledge they were given what was called the "lesser mystery" teaching, some systems call it the "probationary path." After this came the great "Initiations" that were given only to those who had attained the proper strength and purity of character to pass the tests. To gain the great Initiations was the aspiration of the æsthetic and the mystic of all ages, and to assist man to attain the degree of holiness necessary religious homes and communities of all sorts sprang up in every part of the civilized world. While the methods of attaining seem to have varied somewhat in the different religions, the ideal seems to have been the same in all. The object of the discipline was ever to develop the God in man, to subordinate the flesh to the dominion of the Spirit. There seems ever to have been two distinct theories as to the best way to accomplish this; one school taught that only by a perfect knowledge of the law, and by developing a strong will that enabled its possessor to conquer all things, at the last coming into the understanding that only through love can the Buddhic Plane be conquered; and the other extreme taught by the other schools that only by love and devotion and ecstatic communion with God from the first can the victory be won. Methods of training differed according to the ideas of the hierophant in charge of the school.

In all of the ancient religions do we find these ideas, even in their most degenerate stages, although in many cases, now, it is simply a matter of words that have long ago lost their spiritual meaning. The farther back we go, however, the clearer do these teachings stand forth. In the ancient Egyptian religion the Mysteries for ages were most revered. Are we not told that Moses was "learned in all the learning of the Egyptians," as though no higher compliment could be paid him? Plato and Pythagoras, as well as many other of the most notable ancients, have left testimonials as to the virtue of the teachings, having, in many cases taken some of the initiations. In India we find them a recognized part of the ancient Brahmanical, and also of the Buddhic faiths; in Persia they formed a part of the worship of Mithras; there were the mysteries of Samothrace, the Sythian, the Chaldean, the Orphic and Bacchuic Mysteries; and later on the Semi-Mysteries of Greece called the Eleusinian Mysteries; the Delphic, the Phrygian, and many others, including the Mysteries of the Hebrews instituted by Moses; and the "Mysteries of Jesus" taught to the disciples by the Master, often referred to in the New Testament, which were a well-established part of the Apostolic Church, if we may trust the allusions of the early church fathers.

It is interesting to note that the Phrygians, whose Mystery work was most execrated by the orthodox Jew in the day of Christ, were among the very first to recognize in Jesus the Great Master, and that before the first century had elapsed after His death, the nation as a whole had accepted Him as the Messiah. The story is told that in one of their largest cities, early in the second century, not a grown person could be found who was not a professing Christian; so their Mysteries must have prepared them for the truth.

Into the most of these religions in their exoteric ritualism, the most shocking abuses crept during the course of the ages, but these abuses show the degenerative tendency of the crystalizing process through which all religions pass, sooner or later, when confined to their exoteric ritual. On page 88 of his "Christian Creed" Mr. C. W. Leadbeater says: "Never under any circumstances are phallicism and indecency a part of the original conception of a great religion, and the modern theory, that all symbols had primarily some obscene meaning in the minds of the savages who invented them, and that, as in the course of ages, a nation evolved to a higher level, it became ashamed of these cruder ideas and invented far-fetched spiritual interpretations to veil their immodesty, is exactly the reverse of the truth. The great spiritual truth always came first, and it is only after long years, when that has been forgotten, that a degenerate race endeavors to attach a grosser signification to its symbols." Few are so well qualified to testify upon this point, as he has the ability to read the Akasic records, we are told.

When the Mystery teaching was lost to a religion, because of lack of qualified pupils, then invariably the grosser expression of man's nature dominated, even as it is doing in our own religion today, to some extent.

Let us take a hasty glance at the teachings of the Mysteries, so far as they have been given out, for of course, the real secret part of the work is still secret. All that we can obtain is the object to be attained by the methods, not the methods themselves. As explained before, the exoteric Church was expected to produce a thoroughly good man, then, when the realization came to him that nothing is worth while save the service of God and humanity, then was he fit to enter upon the probationary path, or what is called by some the lesser Mysteries, where he put himself through a strict discipline to gain control of the mind, of the senses, and of the will, to develop discrimination, indifference to reward, tolerance, endurance, absence of resentment under unjust treatment, courage to meet the trials of life patiently, and confidence in his Master and in himself. Along with this he was taught something of the history of the Cosmos and the great laws controlling nature. He was shown how Spirit descended into matter, evolving through the lower kingdoms, elemental, mineral, plant, animal, up to the human form, ever pushed by the life of the God within the form, until as a human he receives the baptism, that makes of him a living Spirit, potentially a God.

He was shown that the call had come to him, as an elder brother of the race to prepare himself to teach and guide the rest of humanity, his younger brethren. From this knowledge was born a deeper devotion, a greater love of humanity, and a stronger desire for at-one-ment with the Father.

He was not expected to perfectly attain any of the virtues we have given at this stage, but he was expected to realize fully that they were of all things most desirable, and to be controlled by desire to attain them.

At last the day came when the Great Ones gave him the first Great Initiation, when he was born into the "Kingdom of Heaven." In the cave of the heart was the Christ Child born, of immaculate conception, of the Holy Ghost and virgin, or purified matter ("Mary"), a babe born into the Kingdom, under the star of Initiation, which always rises over the head of the one who is ready, although seen only by those who are psychic. At this birth a very real extension of consciousness ensues, although the individual may not at this time remember the ceremony which is given in the astral body, while the physical lies asleep, yet he can never be the same as though it had not taken place. The God once born cannot die. He may have a hard time, as he will, for many forces will try to destroy Him, but He must survive. He may take ages to work it out, or he may hurry along and make rapid progress, that depends upon himself. The increased consciousness gives him a better understanding than he had before, and better work can be accomplished. The virtues that up to this time he has been struggling to attain must now be perfected. No longer may the faults be controlled, they must be gotten rid of, and the work has that definiteness about it that has not before been required. It may be done in a short time provided the person be sufficiently intense, or it may take many earthly lives to accomplish it. It lies entirely with the individual. The emotional and desire nature must be under complete subjection before the next step can be taken.

But when at last the task is accomplished, the second Great Initiation is given him. Although the work is again given him upon the higher planes, the training that he has received since the first Initiation has so developed his psychic faculties that he is conscious of what is going on at the second Initiation. We are told that the mark of one who is reborn is, that "he asks no higher joy than to feel that he is doing the Master's bidding, he asks no more of the world than that he may serve it;" so the mark of the second Great Initiation, at least in the Bible, seems to be that he receives his new name. He is baptized with water symbolic of the fact that his purification is accomplished, and with fire symbolic of the great spiritual power that is now his.

After this Initiation, with the added power it gives, the progress should be much more rapid, although the temptations of this plane are proportionate to the strength, and each plane has its temptations. Jesus was tempted in the wilderness after the baptism, so all meet the tempter at this stage. But there is a very definite work to be done before higher planes may be reached. As he conquered the desire plane after the first Initiation, so must he now conquer the mental plane, and conquer it so completely that he can function consciously upon the three planes at once, the physical, the astral, and the mental. He must definitely get rid of the illusion of the personal self, realizing that he is not his body, and that his body is but the dress that he wears; that he is not even his astral, or his mental bodies, that they too are but vestures of the real self. He must get rid of doubt, and this can only be accomplished by gaining perfect knowledge. He must forever part with the last trace of superstition. This also is accomplished by mastering knowledge, so the whole struggle of this stage appears to be the mastery of the mental plane.

Then comes the third Great Initiation, the Transfiguration. The man becomes the full-grown Christ, or Master of Compassion. The God completely dominates, so the disciples fall upon their faces, not being able to gaze steadfastly upon his brilliancy. Moses, too, must veil his face when he comes down from the Mount of Initiation. With this initiation comes a power so strong that no unclean thing can live in its pure vibration if allowed to flow in full strength. That it was that felled the lying pair at Peter's feet. Falsehood could not stand the blaze of that aura. That it was that killed the impure hands stretched out to steady the Ark of the Covenant, that symbol of the perfect Man. That it was that caused poor Dagon, the God of the desire nature, to break himself in pieces when placed near to the Ark.

The fourth Great Initiation is the Crucifixion. Here the Initiate must conquer all desire for form, being willing to relinquish it, realizing the Self as One, or he must be willing to crucify the Spirit upon the cross of matter, if by so doing he can assist humanity, forcing his conquering Spirit to stay in a prison house of flesh of his own free will, because of the great love he bears us. Here is a crucifixion of sufficiently heroic proportions to suit the Godlike character of the drama. By His own free will to relinquish the glory that is His, to stay tied to this plane of matter, conscious of all of our sins and sorrows, all through the ages, until He can take us into the Kingdom with Him. This is renunciation of colossal magnitude, for we are taught that naught but His own will can hold the conquering hero down. He is a God and may do what He will. Thus does He give His life for us, His real life, not simply the life of one physical body.

The fifth Great Initiation is the Ascension.

We have used the terms that Biblical students are familiar with, but in other languages they are styled differently, although the idea is the same. In the Bible the student knows that these experiences are all given in connection with the life of Jesus, but many have not noticed that the same typical steps in human life are given in connection with the lives of other Biblical characters. We will show the signs by which they may be discerned as we progress.

We find that all religions have a Great One whom they regard as the first to attain this great distinction, to whom they look for assistance, the "Great Teacher of Gods and men." According to the language is the name used to distinguish Him   To the Hindoo he is the "Bodhisattva" or the "Jagat Gura;" to the Jew he is the Messiah; to the Christian, the Christ; in ancient days the same idea was symbolized by Mithras of the Persians; Orpheus, Bacchus, Dionysius, Apollo of the Greeks; Iacchus, Baal, or Bel and Tamuz of Babylonia; and there are many others, whose names have been so degraded during the ages by the bestial conceptions of undeveloped people, that one needs to dig deeply into the dust of the ages to find the original purity of the thought.

A notable example of this degradation is that of Bacchus, who, because of the wineglass held in the hand of the statue, originally intended to convey the idea that he was about to give a deep draught of the wine of spirituality, preparatory to administering the rite of initiation, which was symbolized by the thyrsus, the rod of initiation which he held in the other hand, became in the course of the ages the God of Revelry. Probably this tendency to degrade the symbolism of a statue was the cause of the law of the Hebrews forbidding the use of images in their worship, and was also the reason that their symbol of the perfect man was the Ark of the Covenant. For the conception of the perfect manifestation of God in man, underlay all of the symbols of the Gods that the people have worshipped at any time in any age. The trouble has been that this conception has varied according to the stage of the evolution of the worshippers and their conception of what perfection was. We Christians have but to turn the pages of history to the Spanish Inquisition, carried on in the name of our Great Master of Compassion, to realize how a noble ideal and a perfect teaching may be degraded and forced to excuse the iniquity in the hearts of men.

This tendency, however, only shows that the people were but infant souls handling a revealed religion that was still beyond their comprehension, except for sporadic instances, here and there, that were sufficient to keep the knowledge of the Mysteries alive upon earth. This, too, explains the necessity of the great secrecy that the initiates were obliged to maintain, and also explains why the Old Testament was to be read to the people by the Priests, who selected such parts as they could understand.

The God that represented this idea to the race was often symbolized to the people by the sun, as being the representative of God upon earth, or by a circle with a diameter through it, symbolic of the dual nature of the creative forces of the Second Person of the Trinity, the positive and negative forces.

Occultism is so little understood by the general reader, that perhaps it would be only just to state here that Occultists recognize in the Christian's Christ, this Great Teacher of Gods and men, but exalt him by claiming that He, and His Great Brother

Buddha, had a hand in founding all of the great religions of the world, giving to the people just so much truth as they could assimilate each time, and reincarnating again and again when the old religion had been so corrupted as to be no longer useful for man's progress, or when it had crystallized into dogma too far to be pliable enough to mould the people. Theosophists are teaching now, that even as he came two thousand years ago, using the body of Jesus to give religion a new impetus, even so is the time now ripe for Him to appear again, and finish the lesson He then started to give the race, namely: the necessity of developing universal brotherly love. They believe that His star has appeared in the east, and that he who tries to give the news to the world, that she may prepare for her King, is best serving the Great One. Whether we believe this or not, it can do no harm to watch events and see what comes.

It certainly looks as though all of the great religions sprang from some common source, and the Great White Lodge, established upon earth by the Great Ones who have man's welfare in mind, gives a probable source. In all of the great religions we trace a great triplicity of helpers, that are typified in our Bible by the Lord Jehovah, the Master Jesus, and the Master Christ; the Lord Jehovah, manifested by Moses guiding man upon the physical plane, Jesus manifesting in Joshua and others teaching man to gain control of the desire nature, and build up the mentality, and then, at last, when the time is ripe for the Christ Child to be born in the heart, the great Christ takes charge of man, and carries him through the great initiations. These three have worked together all through the ages, and others who have attained have worked with them, but in our Bible they are used as the types. Zachariah saw them in his vision of the golden candlestick, "two Great Ones" (Christ and Jesus) who "stand by the Lord of the whole earth." (Lord Jehovah). Zach. IV.

If we may accept the idea that the Great White Lodge exists, then we may accept the idea that the great initiations have been given all through the ages, as fast as a man could be found who was qualified, that it gives them still, and that it will ever continue to give them so long as a man exists who will be helped onward by them. Nations may rise and fall, churches may grow worldly and neglect their part even to the extent of forgetting their Mysteries, but the Great White Lodge may be depended upon not to lose its vigilance for a moment; neither need we fear that the Initiates will ever neglect to do all in their power to draw man onward and upward.

That the early Christians had their "Mysteries of Jesus" is readily seen from the writings of the early Church Fathers, and the New Testament continually uses technical terms used only in Mystery work, as for instance: "babes," "the innocents," the "perfect," the "Brethren." St. Paul speaks very plainly of the Mysteries of the ages being revealed to the saints (not to common church members, note). After getting the information that the Mysteries really existed and had their technical terms and symbols, the pages of the Bible are found to really bristle with references to these typical stages in man's development. The political ambitions of the Church of the fourth and fifth centuries drove the Mystics into retired monasteries, and at last they discontinued their teachings for lack of properly qualified pupils Only here and there could one be found who had the vision celestial, and he was invariably misunderstood and persecuted. The day has now come when it seems to be the intention of the Great Ones to restore the light to the world, and give all Churches a chance to restore the Mysteries to their proper place in ecclesiastical work. When this is done the Churches will find that new life has been infused into their dry bones, and the membership will become a living Spirtual force, fit to be used in the Master's service.

But to return to the uniform teaching of all of the Mystery work of all religions. The thought seems to have been to teach the descent of Spirit into matter, and its evolution upward through seven stages of progress until it appears upon earth as human, into whom the Lord Jehovah breathes the breath of life, and as the Bible states it, *man* became a "living soul." The great law is the law of evolution, evolution of body, evolution of intellect, evolution of soul, because of the impulse given by the vibrations of the God-given Spirit within. In all we find a recognition and acceptance of the great law of cause and effect, or karma, as the Hindoo would express it, but some difference of opinion as to how this law might be expected to work out. In the most of them repeated incarnations of the ego in the flesh seems to be the only legitimate explanation of the problem. So there has grown up the doctrine of reincarnation. In all we find three manifestations of the power of the Supreme, or the Trinity, and in all a recognition of the fact that these three emanate from One Great Source. In all the thought "from God we come to God do we return" is the dominant note, and the enormity of the task of transforming man into a God recognized as demanding more than one life. The methods of the Mystery work being such as was deemed best to enable man to accomplish this transformation as rapidly as possible. In all of the schools good is recognized as the constructive force in nature, and evil as destructive, or error. All recognize, more or less clearly, the creative power of thought.

Mrs. Besant says: "The unity of the moral teachings is not less striking than the unity of the conceptions of the universe, and of the experience of those who rose out of the prison of the body into freedom of the higher spheres. It is clear that a body of primeval teaching was in the hands of definite custodians who in the schools in which they taught had disciples who studied their doctrines. The identity of these schools and their discipline stands out plainly when we study the moral teaching, the demands made on pupils, and the mental and spiritual states to which they were raised."

"And He said, 'unto you it is given to know the mysteries of God, but to others in parables; that seeing they might not see, and hearing they might not understand.'" Luke VIII, 8.

St. Augustine tells us: "That which is called the Christian Religion existed among the ancients, and never did not exist from the beginning of the human race until Christ came in the flesh, after which time the true religion, which already existed, began to be called Christianity." It really seems almost unnecessary to search any farther after such a statement from such a source.

A whole volume might be filled with quotations sustaining my position, but the above, imperfect though it be, must suffice for the present study. All of these things are in print and need not be repeated here.

These similarities all point to a common source, and occultists tell us that that source is the Brotherhood of the Great White Lodge, the hierarchy of Adepts, who watch over and guide the evolution of humanity, and who have preserved these truths unimpaired; from time to time, as necessity arose, reasserting them in the ears of men. From other worlds, from earlier humanities the first Great Ones came to help the child man on our planet, but gradually they have been reinforced by the flower of our own people, until, one by one, the visitors have withdrawn, and we are told that now there is but one of them left, and the work is being done by our own Initiates. So today, the Masters still teach eager pupils, showing the path, and guiding the disciple's steps; still they may be reached by all who seek them bearing the sacrificial fuel of love in their hearts, full of devotion, and unselfish longing to serve; still they carry out the ancient discipline, still unveil the ancient Mysteries. The two pillars of their Lodge gateway are established in strength, for they are Love and Wisdom, and through the straight portal may pass only those from whose shoulders have fallen the burden of selfish desire, in response to the deep-seated devotion to the high ideal.

If all these things be true, a heavy task lies before us: the climb from physical man to the God Man. No wonder the ancients thought many lives in the flesh necessary to give the time needed for the accomplishment of so herculean a task. But what said Christ? "Is it not written in your law, I said ye are Gods, unto whom the word of God came *(and the Scriptures cannot be broken)* say ye of Him whom the Father hath sanctified and sent into the world, Thou blasphemest because I said, I am the Son of God?" John x, 34-35-36.

CHAPTER III.

THE METAPHYSICAL IDEAS OF THE ANCIENT HEBREW.

What were the metaphysical ideas of the ancient Hebrew? That question seems to be one upon which there is a diversity of opinion. Even in the days of Christ in His last incarnation, there were several sects all of whom took their teachings from the Old Testament, and one of them did not believe in the immortality of the soul. The reason for all this ignorance is shown by Christ's question to Nicodemus, "Art thou a Master in Israel and knoweth not these things?" In other words, art thou a Master in Israel, and have not even been born again, in spite of the Mosaic law, that only one who has taken the second Great Initiation shall be a teacher? They had let their Mystery teaching lapse, just as our church today is doing, and, just as it will be with us, they knew not the Lord when He came.

But let us see what we can find to guide us to some sort of a conclusion, for, taking the Bible by itself we do not get a perfect metaphysical scheme of philosophy. There seems to be much taken for granted, probably because the rest was given in the oral Mystery work, and the Great Ones knew that by the time the Scriptures became the property of the masses, that the other world Scriptures would be at their command also. The destiny of the Aryan race is to be so different from the destiny of the races that preceded it, that somewhat different methods must be used to develop the mentality that is to be its crowning acquisition. This race is to develop the intuition also, after the mental is sufficiently developed, so the Mysteries could be hidden under a deeper symbolism, for that faculty will enable the race to find them when the time is ripe. The old race was to learn to obey, the new race is to learn to command. The old race were children, the Aryan race is to attain the manhood of the race. The old race looked to its leaders for everything, the new race is to learn to take care of itself. The old race might be fearful, the new race must be courageous. Fatalism bound the old race, the new race must hear nothing of that. It must be enabled to find that it can conquer all things by its intellectual comprehension of law. The Mysteries must be reserved for it, but must be hidden until it has gained the confidence that comes from experience, and the character that comes from struggle with difficulties, so that the Mystery work may be an assistance, not a drawback

Ephanius Wilson, A M., tells us in "Hebrew Literature": "From the very beginning of their history the Hebrews were a deeply poetic race. They were fully alive to the beauties of external nature, and no national poetry contains more vivid descriptions of the sea, sky, and the panorama of the forest, stream, and mountain, peopled by the varied activities of animated nature. The songs of Zion glow with poetic enthusiasm, but their principal characteristic is their intense earnestness. Yet this religious fervor becomes the basis of sublimity, pathos, and picturesqueness, such as can seldom be approached even by the finest productions of the Attic muse. But the Hebrews were also philosophers, and if they never attained to what we might call the *netteté et clarté* of the Greek metaphysician, they excelled the other thinkers in the boldness and profound spirituality of their philosophical mysticism. In proof of this association we may point to the "Kabbalah."

The word "Kabbalah" means doctrine received by oral tradition, and is applied to these remains to distinguish them from the canonical Hebrew Scriptures. Hebrew speculation attempts in the "Kabbalah" to give a philosophic or theosophistic basis to the Hebrew belief, while at the same time it supplements the doctrines of the Old Testament. The immortality of the soul in the "Kabbalah" is taken for granted, and a complete and consistent psychology is propounded in which is included the Oriental theory of reincarnation. This account of the human soul, as distinct from the human body, treats of the origin and eternal destiny of man's immortal part."

These doctrines are supposed to have been given to Moses on the Mount, and were by him given to Joshua, orally, who in the same manner taught them to the chosen forty who were called receivers. These, in turn, were supposed to give them to such of the people as qualified themselves for the higher knowledge. They were a part of the true Mystery teaching of the Hebrew Religion. Some writers claim that these teachings came from Adam and were handed down to the race by the Divine teachers that instructed infant humanity, and that Moses got his information from Egypt, who had in turn been instructed by Abraham long before. Some claim it started with Abraham, and still others point to the fact that Ezra is admitted to have copied the Books of the Law after the siege of Jerusalem, and they attribute the whole thing to the Babylonian influence upon him. Some think that Ezra wrote only what he remembered of the Law, not changing anything in the least, and the Books of Moses are now just what they were when the Great Leader wrote them, when fresh from the Mount. The Smith Peloubet "Bible Dictionary" says under "Ezra": "The principal works ascribed to Ezra by the Jews are: 1. The institution of the great synagogue; 2. The settling of the Canon of the Scripture, and restoring, correcting, and editing the whole sacred volume; 3. The introduction of the Chaldee character instead of the old Hebrew or Samaritan; 4. The authorship of the books of Chronicles, Ezra, Nehemiah, and some add Esther; and, many of the Jews say, also, of the books of Ezekiel, Daniel and the twelve prophets." Now, how many books have we left in the Old Testament? Only seven—Isaiah, Eccles., Jer., Job, Psalms, Prov., Song of Solomon are all that some one has not attributed to Ezra.

This is very significant if we consider that Ezra lived while the Buddha was teaching in India, and stirring the country to its center, and that he was one of a band of wise men who lived in Babylon on the Cross Roads between India and the Great Sea. Then when we study the symbolism we find the names of Zerubbable (he who was born at the gate of God), Jeshua (Jesus), Noahdiah (Noah beloved of God), who H. P. B. says was Vaivasvatti Manu, also Moses in one incarnation; and Eleazar, who greatly resembles the one whom the Theosophists call Master K. H.; and Meremoth (exalted ones), from the mystical significance of the letters they may be a band of understudies of the Manus, or the Manus of the sub-races. We know that the Great One the Hindoos call the Bodhissattva, and whom we call the Christ, was in incarnation when the Buddha was.

These, with Daniel and his other Initiates, made quite a band of wise men to compile the Sacred Book for the new race.

Ezra v. 2, says "Zerubbable and Jeshua (Jesus) began to build the house of God and with him were the *prophets of God* helping them."

Jeshua, Eleazar, and Meremoth (plural) looked after the furnishing of the temple (religion). The furnishing of a religion would be its Scriptures, of course. The furnishings were to be of Copper and Brass (judgment), Silver (regeneration), and Gold (God's righteousness and wisdom). The Scriptures were to deal with judgment for sin, man's regeneration, and God's wisdom and righteousness.

The Rev. C. D. Ginsburg, LL. D., says in an article entitled "Kabbalah" in the Britannica: "'Kabbalah,' as now used is a technical name for the system of Theosophy which developed among the Jews in the middle ages. In the older Jewish literature the name is applied to the whole body of received religious doctrine with the exception of the Pentateuch, thus including the Prophets and Hagiography as well as the oral traditions, ultimately embodied in the 'Mishna.' It is only since the eleventh and twelfth centuries that the 'Kabbalah' has become the exclusive appellation of the renowned system of Theosophy which claims to have been transmitted uninterruptedly by the mouths of the patriarchs and prophets since the creation of the first man."

Because of the similarities between the doctrines of the "Kabbalah" and those of the "New Testament" many Kabbalists of the highest position in the Synagogue have at different times embraced the Christian faith, and have written elaborate books to bring their Jewish brethren into the Christian Church.

To quote Dr. Wilson exactly, again, for the ideas of the last paragraph are mainly his: "There can be no doubt that the 'Kabbalah' contains the ripest fruit of spiritual and mystical speculation which the Jewish world produced on subjects which had hitherto been obscured by the gross anthropomorphism of such men as Maimonides and his school. We can understand the revolt of devout Hebrews from traditions which represented Jehovah as wearing a phylactery, and as descending to the earth for the purpose of taking a razor and shaving the head of Sennacherib. The theory of the Sephiroth was at least a noble and truly reverent guess" (if guess it was) "at the mode of God's immanence in nature. This conception won the favor of the Christian philosophers in the middle ages and indeed was adopted by the angelic Dr. Aquinas himself, the foremost of ecclesiastical and scholastic metaphysicians. The psychology of the 'Kabbalah,' even with its treatment of the soul's pre-existence before union with the body, found many advocates among Gentile and even Christian philosophers."

"We are therefore led to the conclusion that the 'Kabbalah' is by far the most exalted, the most profound, and the most interesting of all the mass of traditional literature which comprises among other writings, such remains as the 'Targums' and the 'Talmuds'."

I have quoted at length from these two eminent scholars that the reader may have freshly in mind the probable conceptions of the ancient Hebrew, that rendered plain to him so much that has troubled us in our endeavor to understand the Old Testament.

We must remember that the Jew was not only an Oriental in the fact that he lived in Palestine, but he was an Oriental in the fullest sense of the term in his earlier history, having come originally from the north of India, and belonging to the race that had escaped from the flood of Atlantis, from which the Hindoo race had evolved. Theosophists claim that the tribe that gave us the Jews of today were set aside, or taken apart, to start the new Fifth Race along higher lines by the Manu, who H. P. B. says was Noah; so a large part of their earlier emigrations must have been through the plains and mountains of India, as they traveled southwestwardly down into Chaldea, where they stayed for long ages, drinking in the religious ideas of the people. We see this continually cropping out in the allegories, many of which date from this period in their wanderings, and are located in the far east rather than in Palestine. The local coloring being given later on by Ezra to cultivate the patriotism of the Jews. Consequently it was quite natural that the Jew should have had much the same idea of the ancient truths as were held by the Indians and Babylonians, especially as their patriarchs were very evidently Initiates. We are told that Abraham went into Egypt with Lot, and that Moses had "all of the learning of the Egyptians," which could mean nothing less than that he had studied in the great school located there, that was so famous for so many ages, under the rule of the Great White Lodge.

A literal reading of the Scriptures shows Daniel to have been a wise man, or one of the Magi, a high Initiate, and he and his companions are shown as performing miracles. We are told they were the wisest of all the wise men. Naturally a book compiled at such a time under such supervision (for we are told Ezra rewrote) must have been the best that could be compiled for the new race that was to need it. Surely it is worth while to study it carefully.

We should remember that an allegory is a story, historical or otherwise, used to carry a spiritual or poetic meaning. The stories selected are usually historical because the historical significance makes the meaning clearer. Ezra selected the stories that were no doubt well known in his day, to convey this inner meaning. The most of the allegories show evidence of their Aryan origin, but as the Jews were to be the custodians of the Scriptures during so many ages, they were to be inspired with loyalty by the stories being given a local coloring.

Their Initiates understood. The priests read such portions of the Scripture to the people as they were able to understand. This worked all right so long as the Priesthood were Initiates. It is only after the Mysteries are lost that the priesthood can be no longer trusted to guide the people.

Let us see if we can put in a few words the great scheme of things that is given in the Kabbalah, and the Mishna, for without these the Old Testament must ever be misunderstood, as it takes so much knowledge for granted on the part of the reader that can be supplied from no other source.

Great hierarchies of forces are sometimes referred to in the Bible, showing that the great plan was understood; but the teaching as a whole is concise, and concerns generally just what is needed for the practical training of the race.

They show that, first, there is "The Most Holy Ancient One," the "Concealed of all Concealments," as the Kabbalah quaintly puts it; then in common with all great religions they have their Trinity of manifestations in their "Kether" (crown), the I, Yod, the Father of the Christian, the First Logos of the Theosophist, the will manifestation of the "Most Holy Ancient One."

Second, they have "Chokmah (wisdom), the H, Hevah, the Second Logos of the Theosophist, the Son of the Christian, the Divine woman of the Old Testament.

Third, comes Binah (understanding), VH, The Holy Spirit of the Christian, the Third Logos of the Theosophist.

From understanding born of God's creative love and wisdom come forth seven (Sephiroth), the seven attributes of God manifesting upon the seven planes.

We are shown that everything in nature has a triune manifestation in its possibilities. First, this applies to the Cosmos, to our Universe, to our planet, then to man. A scheme very simple, yet one of infinite possibilities. All showing a triune manifestation of the seven attributes of God. In man it shows in his moral, mental, and spiritual natures. He is ever pictured as being "made in the image of God."

IHVH, which has been translated Jehovah in our Bible in the new version, and God in the old one, seems to be intended to indicate these three great streams of creative power on their downward course into matter.

"The Most Holy Ancient One" is symbolized as the "Vast Countenance." The Vast Countenance has but one side, because with him all things are right; hence we have but one "all-seeing eye."

The Kabbalah says when the Vast Countenance uncovers towards the little countenance (man) all things are beheld in the light of mercy. Wrath and judgment cometh forth from the little countenance, for the little countenance showeth two sides, both the right and the left.

"When it is written, My wrath is kindled, the wrath of Tetragrammaton is kindled, etc., is to be understood to refer to the little countenance (Microprosopus)." P. 198 "Kabbalah."

"War cometh from the wrath of Microprosopus" (Man).

"The fire of war is not mitigated save by the fire of the Altar." "Kabbalah," P. 198.

"The one 'Yod' is concealed, the other is made manifest, but that which is hidden and that which is manifest are balanced by equilibrium of forms." P. 92, "Kabbalah."

"The Mother 'H' is joined unto the king and is found to form one body with Him." P. 75.

"When the male is joined with the female they both form one complete body." P. 334, "Kabbalah."

"The path of the bride 'H' is called the land of Canaan wherein Joshua found giants." (It is in the lower planes where the wisdom creative outflow makes bodies and creates forms of all kinds.) P. 334, "Kabbalah."

"When the inferior man descendeth into this world, like unto the Supernal form, in himself there are found two Spirits. Man is formed from two sides, from the right and from the left. P. 91, "Kabbalah."

"With respect unto the right side he had the Holy Intelligences; with respect to the left side, the animal soul." Here is the animal that man is commanded to sacrifice.

Page 316, paragraph 565: "Hence it is written (Gen. VIII, 21). And IHVH smelled a sweet savor. It is not written, He smells the odor of sacrifice. What is sweet save rest? Assuredly the Spirit at rest is the mitigation of the Lords of judgment. When therefore it is said that IHVH smelled the odor of rest, most certainly the odor of the sacrificed victim is not meant; but the odor of those mitigations of severity which are referred to the nose of "Microprosopus" (Man).

"From the nose of Microprosopus (Man) proceedeth from the one nostril smoke and fire, and from the other peace and beneficient Spirits. From the Kabbalah as translated by S. L. Mac Gregor Mathers in "Kabbalah Unveiled."

To quote a few lines of the "Kabbalah" as translated by Dr. Wilson: "The 'Most Holy Ancient One' is found to have three heads, which are contained in one head. (His manifestation is triune.) And he Himself is that only highest Supreme Head."

"And since He the Most Holy Ancient One is thus symbolized in the triad all other lights which shine are included in triads."

Moreover the Most Holy Ancient One is symbolized by the duad (positive and negative), so also all the remaining lights are mystically divided into duads."

"Furthermore the 'Most Holy Ancient One' is symbolized and concealed under the conception of unity, for He Himself is One and all things are one."

So Moses said to the people, "Hear, Oh Israel, There is one God; Him only shalt thou worship." He wanted to inculcate in them the understanding of the unity that it is the destiny of the Aryan race to understand.

The Hindoo loved deep metaphysical speculation, but the Aryan race was to live an active life, and the great secrets of the beginning of things are given in a few terse words in Genesis. First, the perfect thought form of Elohim is given in Ch. I, then in Ch. II, beginning with fourth verse, we see the great Lord Jehovah starting humanity on its evolutionary path on this planet, by which it may attain the perfection foreseen in the first chapter when God saw it and it was *Good*.

The Theosophists tell us that our humanity evolved up to the human form upon the Moon chain, and the Bible shows that the egos were human, because the Lord Jehovah made a body for Man. He was already man and the Lord Jehovah makes him a body of the dust, or finer, etheric, particles of the lower planes, or mental matter.

This will be brought out more fully in other chapters, but the first glimpse given us is so very brief, that one must turn to other Scriptures to get a full conception of the depth of meaning of the cryptic phrases. A deep study, however, shows that they contradict no scientific fact that has been proven, nor do they contradict other Scriptural accounts. It is all there, but it is evidently not the work of the Aryan race to dwell upon that great beginning so much as to consider the path he is to take to attain to the greatest degree of usefulness. The typical steps of the race in their progress is well marked out, and, if we study the symbolic meaning of the allegories we will find a clear story of the great plan of the Infinite for our salvation, which is a story of evolution; and the hopeful part of it is, that we are given time enough to accomplish it.

In this entirely inadequate review the writer has endeavored to give the reader a few of the facts that throw light upon the inner meaning of the Scriptures of the Hebrew (those who have crossed over), and in the succeeding chapters will bring out other points that will help, as the interpretation of passages call for them.

CHAPTER IV.

THE STORY OF CREATION.

Although many of these points are brought out in some of the other chapters, perhaps it would be wise to give a connected account of the creation in as few words as possible, as it reads symbolically, as so many have had serious trouble with these first few chapters of our Bible.

All translators seem to agree that there are two accounts of the creation given in Genesis, and that the one in the second chapter seems to be by far the older of the two. It seems very probable that the first chapter was not written until the Great Ones met in Babylon in the time of Ezra to compile the Scripture for the new Aryan race. As was fitting in a work of that kind, in a few terse sentences the origin of things was shown.

From occult sources we learn that all things that appear upon the Physical Plane must first appear upon the Mental Plane. To make the statement so plain that it may be readily grasped by a mind that has not studied along these lines, no house, or anything else, can be built until it has been clearly planned in the mind of the architect. As he conceives of this plan and perfects it in his mind he builds it upon the Mental Plane. God's thoughts are supposed to rest upon the Cosmic Mental Plane. When the Builder needs them we are told that He brings them down.

So in the first chapter of Genesis we find the perfected thought form of the Logos (God) in his seven-fold expression, showing the perfected patterns of all the seven great kingdoms of nature, as they will ultimately become when their evolution is complete.

The Kabbalah gives us the key to this in the words "Moses was perfect from the very day of his birth, seeing it is written, Ex. II, 2. 'And she saw him that he was good.'" Page 197, paragraph 694. If the mother of Moses pronouncing him good meant that he was perfect from his birth, and Occultists tell us this was indeed true, as he was perfected upon the Moon Chain, then how much more certain is it that when God looked upon his creations and pronounced them good it meant that they were present to His mind as they were to become when the whole course of their long evolution shall have been accomplished. Is it not reasonable to suppose that it was the perfected pattern that He pronounced good? We certainly realize that at the present stage there is nothing perfect. All is in a stage of evolution towards perfection.

In "Inner Life," Vol. II, page 162, Mr. Leadbeater says: "The Logos has thought out the whole life of His system, not only as it is now, but as it has been every moment in the past, and as it will be every moment in the future. And His thought calls into existence that of which He thinks. These thought forms are said to be on the Cosmic Mental Plane,—two whole sets of seven planes above our set of seven. Thus we may say that on the Cosmic Mental Plane the whole system was called into existence simultaneously by that thought,—an act of special creation."

Let us look at that word "Elohim," the word that is translated God, or Jehovah, according to the version. Elohim is a feminine noun with a masculine plural ending, and might be translated abstractly, power and creative wisdom; or it may mean the great creative agents of the Infinite At any rate, it is plural.

In the first chapter we find Elohim creating, and in the second chapter it is the Lord Jehovah who is carrying on the work. However the word bârâ (create) is used but three times in the first chapter of Genesis: first as to the origin of matter, second as to the origin of life, and third as to the origin of man's soul. All other things are said to be made (re-formed).

In spite of the most determined efforts the scientists have not been able to prove the stages of creation as given in Genesis I to be erroneous. They practically agree with the nebular hypothesis as worked out scientifically. First, "In the beginning Elohim created." Science has nothing to say about that beginning. Second, fine gaseous matter, too fine to reflect light; third, gas condenses into liquid; fourth, light, liquid reflects light; fifth, mist rises from the water and a space is left between the water above, and the water below; sixth, great upheavals of land; seventh, grass, herbs, fruit trees; eighth, the mist gets less dense, and the sun, moon, and stars appear; ninth, living creatures begin to swarm in the waters and birds begin to fly; tenth, cattle and beasts of the field; eleventh, Man; twelfth, God. (The Hebrew always begins and ends with God.) This is now generally conceded as the probable sequence of events.

But in reading this inner story forget all about days of twenty-four hours each, and read "evening of inharmony and morning of harmony to God's will, one day, or one period of time. There is no time upon the Plane where these thought forms of Divinity lie. Great periods of time are involved all now know, but how much time can never be known until the end. Science and Occultism have forced the narrow minded to accept the truth in regard to the great periods of time that must have elapsed, to have accomplished so much as has been done, so far, in the great evolutionary march, but it is impossible for the human mind to conceive of the periods involved.

The first chapter ending with the third verse of the second chapter gives us the perfected thought form of the Great Architect of the Universe, complete even to the smallest detail of what the destiny of the planet and all of its multitudinous creatures shall be when they shall have completed their long evolutionary journey.

In the second chapter, beginning with the fourth verse, we find the Great Master Builder, the Lord Jehovah, beginning His work, for to Him was given the great task of starting the evolutionary march. The symbol of this Great One is always the Moon. Occultists tell us He was the Regent of the great Moon Chain. "Perfect from His birth," He is the Seed Manu of the Theosophist.

The Lord Jehovah's first work is to give to man a body in which to manifest. We find the egos of humanity lying upon the Buddhic Plane. They are already human, having reached that stage of evolution upon the Moon Chain. The Lord Jehovah builds man a body of the dust (the Kabbalah says "of the finer etheric matter," evidently of the mental matter). He forms the body out of the atomic matter of the Mental Plane but must call upon the second breath, or Spirit, or the Second Great Outpouring before it can become a "Living Soul," not a physical body.

The first breath was given when Elohim breathed upon the face of the waters, and impregnated all matter with the Holy Spirit and brought forth the atomic structure of all planes, but no forms can be brought forth without the attractive force of the

THE STORY OF CREATION

Great Second Outpouring of Spirit. The egos (for it is all in the plural, and refers to humanity) are now ready to function on the Mental Plane. They have causal and mental bodies.

Lord Jehovah places humanity in a garden of trees. Trees are symbols of teachers of wisdom. The garden is eastward, or toward intellectuality. The most of the teachers teach that it is best to learn by obedience to God's law, but one teaches that by breaking law will experience be gained more rapidly. Man is to be a free will being, so he must be given a choice. The Lord Jehovah warns and guides, but does not force.

Four rivers flow out of Eden, the Wisdom Plane, "for there is a Superior Eden" we are told in the Kabbalah, "and an Inferior Eden," and that "Eden" means "Chokmah" (wisdom), so the four rivers are rivers of wisdom, to water the four planes for the development of humanity. Pishon means sinking into a cleft, and is the one that waters the plane next to the one on which Eden is situated. Inferior Eden is on the Mental Plane, so Pishon must water the Astral. Gihon, the rushing roaring river, waters the Physical Plane, or the land of Cush, the black land. Hiddikel, we are told by the Bible Dictionary, is a river in Paradise, and so it is, for it waters the Mental Plane or the land of Assyria (Asshur son of Shem, Shem the Christ of the fourth root race). Euphrates, the great and abounding river, waters the Buddhic Plane, or the Universal Love Plane, the Plane of Unity.

Here is the Promised Land of the race. The conquest of these four planes is to be its destiny, and this is the Promised Land always referred to in Scripture.

"In the day that thou eatest" of the fruit of the tree of good and evil (try to learn by breaking law), "thou shalt surely die," or a better translation is, "thou shall lead a dying life," warns the good Lord Jehovah.

In the rib story we find the Lord Jehovah providing an Astral body for humanity, and again He calls upon the Second Great Outpouring before the body can be made. This time the symbolism is somewhat different. The letter "Yod" is the symbol of the first person of the Trinity, also of the Monad. The shape of the letter "Yod" is something like a rib with a piece of the vertebra attached. The symbol is this: Adam was one "Yod," and the Lord Jehovah took another "Yod," or a Second

Outpouring of the Infinite at the side of Adam, and closed up the rent thereof. That is "Yod" joined to "Yod" makes the letter H, "Hevah," the symbol of the Second Great Outpouring. This word "Hevah" is translated "Eve" and really means the creative love wisdom manifestation, or the Second Outpouring, the form producing outpouring upon any plane. The Lord Jehovah called this production woman (Isshah) "whom God lends," or as one translator puts it "the completion of man." In other words, a body for man (humanity) to function in.

Speaking of the Second Great Outpouring, Mr. Leadbeater, on page 30 of "Christian Creed," small edition, says: "On the downward arc of its mighty curve it simply aggregates round itself the different kinds of matter on the various planes, so that all may be accustomed and adapted to act as its vehicles."

The "Kabbalah" says, page 334: "When the male is joined with the female they both constitute one complete body," and again, "when the Masculine and Feminine are joined together they appear to form only one body, and this is Arcanum"; again, "The Mother H is joined to the King and is found to form one body with him."

So evidently this episode is simply showing the providing of an Astral vehicle for the race to function in.

"He shall leave his father and his mother" (the creative forces that have brought him here), "and cleave" to his Eve, his vehicles that he has entered, till he gets control of them.

But he and his body were naked (of experience).

Now comes the tempter, through this new strong desire body which is full of craving for sensation. Tame obedience does not give it the thrills it wants.

The serpent is a symbol of wisdom. The brazen serpent is true wisdom; the black serpent, black art; but it always refers to wisdom of some sort, or a great teacher of some sort. So this teacher shows the young race how to get sensation by breaking law.

The "Kabbalah" says: "When the inferior man descendeth (into this world) like unto the Supernal form (in himself) there are found two spirits, so that man is formed from two sides, from the right side and from the left side. With respect to the right side he hath the Holy Intelligences, with respect to the left side he hath the animal soul." (Here is the animal man was commanded to sacrifice.)

So when Adam said to Lord Jehovah, "The woman Thou gavest me she did it," he simply meant, this new body that You gave me, she did it and passed the experience on to me her higher self.

By breaking the law humanity finds themselves so naked of experience that they know not what to do next, so they hide from Lord Jehovah in fear. Breaking the law has also blinded their clear sight upon the higher planes. When the Lord Jehovah comes they can see Him but faintly, and it seems as though the dusk of evening had settled down upon them, as indeed it had, because by breaking law they have densified matter and soon their sight of those higher planes will be cut entirely off.

In the curse of the serpent we see the distinct cleavage of the Mental Plane. There will ever be a lower and a higher Mental Plane. although in a sense they are really one. The serpent, or teacher, or the Wisdom, is represented as creeping when manifesting upon the lower Mental Plane. Of dust shall she eat, or of mental matter, and Humanity will now gain wisdom only as he stumbles over the serpent in hidden places and feels the pain of the experience.

Unto woman, or the desire body (remember woman is the manifestation of the Second Person of the Trinity upon any plane), "Thy desire shall be to thine husband" or thy higher self ("Thy maker is thine husband") "and he shall rule over thee."

Unto Adam, "cursed" (or bound by the law of cause and effect), "is the ground for thy sake." That is, since you will have it so, you will have to learn to conquer this plane according to law. "In sorrow shalt thou eat of it, in the sweat" (or emanations) "of thy head shalt thou eat bread till thou return to the ground, for dust thou art, to dust shalt thou return." That is, by intellectual comprehension must he learn to get his bread according to law, for of dust, or of mental matter is he made, and to the Mental Plane must he return. And Humanity called his wife's name Eve because she was "the mother of all living," in the sense that she was the H, Hevah, the symbol of the Second Great Outpouring, the form producing outpouring, as stated elsewhere. ("In the beginning was the word and the word was with God and the word was God. Without Him was not anything made that was made.", John I, 1. This is the great woman of Scripture. The great creative Love Wisdom Out Flow no matter where manifested. In this case it manifested as vehicles in which man could manifest.

Humanity by gratifying desire, has sunken into animal bodies or, perhaps I should say, physical bodies. These bodies have been evolving up from the animal kingdom, so Lord Jehovah does not make any new ones now; He only wraps about them the skins of animals, their own skins, or circumscribes their development.

H. P. B. says that the first men were very fluidic, but the day came when their development was definitely checked by a thickening of the outer layers of the atoms of their bodies. I am not attempting to quote exactly, as I have not the book at hand.

Man was driven out of the Garden of Eden by his own rebellion against law, and will only be able to return when by ages of experience he learns how to be able to grasp the handle of the sword of spiritual truth that he might have had by abiding in the law all of the time.

And humanity knew Eve (became accustomed to his new vehicles), and they conceived and bare Cain Abel the dual-natured first really physical race, H. P. B. tells us.

When Eve, the vehicle of humanity, brought forth the child she said, "I have gotten a man with IHVH"; that is, I have gotten a man with the Spirit of God within.

Abel means Spirit, and Cain means Possessor. It is the dual-natured humanity. The first human race is born. Abel, the spiritual nature of man, naturally becomes a keeper of sheep or a teacher of the more evolved, and would gladly put his animal nature upon the altar in service to God; but Cain, the strongly physical Cain, will offer up the first fruits of the earth, or anything else, but his animal nature, never. When the Spirit within remonstrates he kills his Abel (Spirit) and buries it beneath the earth, or his dense physical. His animal propensities are in the ascendant.

The curse is, because he has done this thing the natural law of cause and effect will force him to be a wanderer in the land; that is, he will have to reincarnate many times in the physical body, and wander upon the Physical Plane, until he learns the lesson that his animal nature is his reasonable offering to God. It will take him ages to learn this lesson, hence the necessity of reincarnation.

He dwelt in the land of Nod (wandering) on the east of Eden, on the side of intellectual understanding.

And Cain knew his wife (became used to his new bodies), and brought forth a new sub race called Enoch, and the race Cain built a city and called it Enoch after the new sub race.

Hindoo writings say that when the bodies were ready the most evolved of the egos who were coming down into incarnation refused to use them, and then the mindless ones rushed in. Probably these are the ones referred to in the Bible by the race Cain. It was no doubt the great Lemurian race.

That these are the people is shown by that quaint old allegory of Lamech and his two wives (physical and astral bodies), Adah (ornament, physical body), Zellah (shadow, or astral body). Adah bare such as dwell in tents (have bodies), and Zillah bare Tubal Cain, the forger of every cutting instrument of brass, and iron, or every instrument of destruction and judgment. Through desire cometh judgment and destruction. In this little poem we see violence ushered in.

In Seth we have the great fourth root race. For nine hundred and thirty years these egos kept dropping into incarnation, and now men began to call upon Jehovah.

In the genealogy of Seth that follows may be discerned the seven sub-races of the fourth root race, but space forbids our handling it at this time.

CHAPTER V.

SIGNIFICANCE OF THE GENEALOGY OF SHEM, AND THE WORK OF ABRAHAM AND LOT.

In the genealogy, by looking up the meaning of the personal nouns, we find a very different story told than the one seen at first sight. We have not the time to trace them at length, but note that Japheth settles the Coast Lands and becomes the traders of the race, the intellectual, material, strongly practical people.

The sons of Ham settle in the Land of Shinar (the Land of Two Rivers). Two rivers symbolize the consciousness of the people.

The reader will remember that of the four rivers of Wisdom that flowed from the Garden of Eden, the two lower watered the Physical and Desire planes, so the people designated Ham live upon only the Physical and Emotional Plane.

The allegory of the Tower of Babel (Gate of God) brings this out.

The whole earth, we are told, were of one language (they understood the symbolic language), so the people of the Land of Two Rivers (Shinar) at once tried to discover the Mysteries for themselves although they had only brick (hardened physical natures) for stone (Masters of Compassion) and slime (low physical desires) had they for mortar (which should be universal love and wisdom). So they were deprived of the knowledge of the symbolic language to prevent their injuring themselves by handling holy things with impure hands, and bringing upon themselves the destruction that Atlantis had suffered for the same fault.

We will trace the line of Shem, the second sub-race, as it gradually evolved during the ages.

Remember Shem means "the name," and the race that descended from this line were the priestly class. The name of Shelah means petition or prayer, and from prayer is begotten

SIGNIFICANCE OF THE GENEALOGY OF SHEM

Eber, or Heber, those who crossed over, or developed the new race characteristics. In Peleg we see division, the two races became markedly different, or possibly a new sub-race appears. Serug, a branch, begets Nahor, a snorter, a name sometimes used in India today for Yoga, and the Yoga begets Terah, which means station, or stopping place.

We find Terah lives two hundred and fifty years in idolatry. Idolatry means the worship of an image. Man is made in the image of God, so idolatry meant primarily worship of self, or selfishness.

Terah, this stopping place of selfishness, begets Abram, exalted father; Nahor, another Yoga, and Haran, a mountaineer, or high Initiate, one high in spirituality.

Ur means God or light, Chaldea means intellectuality; so when Abram was called from Ur of Chaldea he was called from the God of the intellect and goes to the land of Canaan (land of humility, low-lying land). From this land of humility he gradually mounts to Haran, or the spiritual heights, at which time Lord IHVH appears to him; Terah follows Abram to Haran but he dies on the spiritual heights—he cannot stand that altitude. Lord Jehovah, on the Manu, the manifestation of IHVH, appears to him and enters into an agreement with him that his seed shall cover the earth, but he must leave his kindred, or the stopping place of material intellectuality.

Lot means wrapped in a veil or covering. He is the son of Haran the High Initiate, the grandson of Bethuel, the dweller in God, and nephew of the Yoga, Nahor. Lot evidently refers to the esoteric branch of a great religious system, as well as to the great hierophant who led it. Just who this Great One was I have not been able to quite determine from the information given us in the Bible, but if Abraham is Master Moro, then Lot must be Master Koot Hoomi, for Mr. Leadbeater shows those two leading great emigrations of the race southward in the "Lives."

Legend tells us that Abram was a great prince. Some of the Legends of ancient Damascus claim that he at one time ruled that city for a time, coming along with an army and stopping quite a number of years, then taking his people he departed as he had come. The Arab and Mohammedan generally, believe that Abraham was one of their great leaders. To this day they call him

El Khalil, friend of God. H. P. B. says Abram means no-Brahman, and also says he was a Manu, but does not state which Manu. It looks as though he were an understudy of the Great Manu, and I believe I am right in assuming that he is the same ego as we today reverence as Master Moro, the Manu of the coming sixth root race.

To be sure, this demands that we shift the scene of Abraham's activities farther east than we have been wont to think of them, but this reading shows that these people really were living in the eastern or middle rather than western Asia.

Lot, the Bible tells us, went with Abraham, the great leader of the people; and so did Sarah, his sister wife, or his inner school of wisdom or inner consciousness—at any rate, Mystery work of some sort. But, says some one, that is too far-fetched. My friend, turn to Gal. IV, 24, and on, "For it is written that Abraham had two sons, one by the handmaid, and one by the free woman * * * " Which things contain an allegory; for these women are two covenants, the one bearing children to the flesh and the other bearing children of the Spirit. I have used this quotation in another place, but there is no other quite so pertinent to the case in hand.

Epiphanius Wilson, A. M., in his "Hebrew Literature," page 22, says: "The Talmud says, 'Abraham is said to have put Sarah into a box when he brought her into Egypt, that none should see her beauty. At the custom house toll was demanded. Abraham said he was ready to pay. The custom house officer said, "Thou bringest bales?" He said, "I will pay for bales." They said, "Thou bringest gold?" He said, "I will pay for gold." They said, "Silk?" He said, "I will pay for silk." They said, "Thou bringest pearls?" He said, "I will pay for pearls." They said, "Thou must open the box"; whereon her splendor shown over the whole land of Egypt.' " Another version of this same story runs that Sarah flew out of the box and settled over all the land as a white mist, and Egypt was never the same again. Evidently it was well understood at one time that Sarah was not a woman but had something to do with Mystery work and Divine Wisdom.

So Abraham, Lot, and Sarah and all the *"souls"* (notice, not *"bodies"*) that they had gotten in Haran, the spiritual heights, go by the land of Canaan, or humiliation, to the place of Shechem, or mountain ridge of spiritual exaltation, to the "Oak of Moreh," which means strong and exalted teacher.

Here again, while on the spiritual heights, under a great teacher, IHVH appears to Abram, and promises him material blessings—all the land and the nations to cover it—all that Lord Jehovah could promise, as said before, for that was his part of the work of the Supreme—to look after the material welfare of the new race. Abram now erects an altar to Lord Jehovah—the Manu—the God of cause and effect, or he establishes a religion in which the great law of cause and effect is the key note, an eye for an eye, a tooth for a tooth. As a man soweth so must he also reap. The Hindoo calls this the law of Karma, and the Theosophist does likewise, it being a brief way of putting it.

If you will look at the map of Palestine you will see that Ai and Bethel lie almost due north and south of each other, so that to camp with one on the east and the other on the west would be a physical impossibility. They were probably given their names from this very allegory. After having this religious experience we find Abraham pitching his tent, having Ai (heap of ruins) the effete fourth root race upon the east, and Bethel (the Temple of the Living God, or the perfected Man) on the west. He is dwelling between the last degenerate race and the future possibilities of the new race. And so we often find the patriarchs camping between Ai and Bethel, no matter where they may be, nor where they are going. Here again he builds an altar, or he sets up his religion in every camp he makes. He encourages religion wherever it is.

There was a sore famine in that land, we are told; this refers to spiritual famine in this reading. They go down into Egypt. When they go down into Egypt it is a symbol of seeking the higher wisdom, for the Great White Lodge existed there for ages, and was sought by all who aspired to the higher learning; but when we find them in bondage to Egypt it means bondage of sin and ignorance, bondage to the land of Cush, the black land, or the physical. This time they are going after food (spiritual food). I cannot take the time to follow them upon this trip, but keep in mind that Sarah is simply the Mystery work, his higher consciousness, that Abraham wants to hide from the Egyptians. He wants her to appear as his sister, that is, does not want to admit how much he does know, wants his wisdom to appear as belonging to one of the lower classes; but the Egyptians discover his merits and would keep him. That was the custom of these schools; they tried to keep all the great hierophants in connection with their own school if they could, and the great school of Egypt is often called a "harlot" because of this propensity to accept truth from any source and make it her own.

Very evidently Abraham and Lot and their followers went to Egypt to study. Occultists tell us that this great school was established before the destruction of Atlantis, and for ages and ages remained in the hands of the White Brotherhood, but some authorities say that at last it became corrupt and the Great Ones were obliged to withdraw from it, and Egypt became the home of black art. Mr. Leadbeater, however, speaks as though the Great White Lodge was still there.

After leaving Egypt Abraham starts south, or towards the Spirit,—south symbolizes Spirit,—and again pitches his tent between Ai and Bethel, although miles south of the geographical position of the towns called by those names, between the past and the future possibilities of the race, and they have great possessions (spiritual possessions).

Abram, remember, is the understudy of the Manu, and he is the great Law Giver of the people, the leader of the exoteric part of the religion, the leader of the masses. Lot, on the other hand, is in charge of the higher Mystery work, out of which the Initiates are to come. You will notice in the account that Abram sees angels and gets messages from God only when near great teachers (oaks at Mamre), while Lot sees and recognizes the angels at once that Abram entertained unawares. They were obliged to reveal their character to Abram; Lot knew them. Abram served them with the feast that symbolized the physical; Lot fed them on unleavened bread, the diet of the æsthetic. Abram's wife, or inner work, is barren,—brings forth no Initiates,—he is too active upon the Physical Plane trying to help the race. The leaders of Lot's people, or his herdsmen, and the leaders of Abram's people strive together, the exoteric and the esoteric sections cannot agree. This struggle has been common all through the ages, the blind always want the angels first, before they have developed the sight to perceive them when they do come.

SIGNIFICANCE OF THE GENEALOGY OF SHEM

Because of the strife between their followers, the great leaders in perfect amity decide to part, and Abraham says, "Take your choice, your work is the most important. If you go one way then will I go the other. Our work is diametrically opposite; I am working with IHVH descending, while it is your duty to guide it to conquest over the matter that I am helping to wrap about it. You ascend on the way back to the Father; I must see to the descending current. Both of us are children of the same Father, therefore let us not strive, for are we not brethren?" So each applies himself to his own work and they separate, in perfect friendliness.

Lot decides to settle in the plains watered by the Jordan (the descending torrent) or the torrent of degenerate tendencies of the old race, in the cities of the plain, thinking, no doubt, that here he may do good with his work; but the people, while they welcome him warmly, want the angels handed out to them at once. That is, they want to be taught white magic. Lot tells them, "Here are my daughters" (or his two lower classes). Study in them the allotted time and then you may hope for the higher work; but no, they will have the angels, but when they come up against the house they find themselves blind. They cannot see the angels because of their gross natures.

You will note that Lot has the three degrees of work, wife, and two daughters, and he seems to be able to talk to the angels. (He has occult training.) The angels advise Lot to seek a more retired spot for his work, and they leave the city, and seek the mountains for more quiet, or more safety while prosecuting his work upon higher planes. They start under the impulse given by the heavenly visitants, but Lot's wife, or his highest class of workers, his most consecrated ones, look back and are turned into a pillar of salt. Now salt means preservative, and pillar means a support of a structure, so a school of preservative wisdom supporting the Temple of Truth was left upon the edge of the land while the inhabitants were being consumed by the fire and brimstone of their own lust and material desires.

Lot retires to the Cave of Initiation in the mountains after staying in Zoar, or city of humiliation, for a time, and his lower degree workers persuade him to take of the wine of spiritual ecstasy, and to go in to him separately because they are in different degrees of work, and they study with him, or "lie with him"—we have an echo of this usage in our "I lay to it till I accomplished it—till they become one with him, or a wife to him, in wisdom, and are able to bring forth sons of wisdom, Initiates. One of them begets the great race called Moab, which at first was a school of wisdom that was named "Like unto his father," or like unto Lot, the greatest Hierophant of his times, and the other Benami, the father of Ammon, the spiritual mountaineer, sons of renown, or High Initiates, those upon the heights of spirituality. So here in the dawn of historic time we find a sweet story of love and self-sacrifice that makes one's heart beat with renewed courage because of the assurance that the race has never been without a father, nor have the loving elder brothers ever been absent from the earthly family circle. Always have there been the younger children who have had their naughty spells, but ever have the loving elders cared for them, ever have they been guided, ever have there been schools to train them as soon as they would take the teaching. Does this not leave a sweeter taste in the mouth than the old reading that you were obliged to skip when the children were listening?

CHAPTER VI.

NOAH AND THE FLOOD.

"The Theosophist notes in the study of a religion three elements: one due to primitive and faulty conceptions of natural phenomena; second, an element of fundamental truth which was implanted in it by a great religious teacher; and, third, a theology raised on both long after the days of the founder of the religion. Noting these three elements in a religion, the Theosophist continually searches for the second group of ideas, and when he finds these he finds that they are not so radically different from the same element to be found in the other religions."—*C. J. in Primer of Theosophy.*"

In the story of the Creation and the Flood the faulty conception of natural phenomena has led to many serious misunderstandings, and the foolish chronology foisted upon the unsuspecting world by well-meaning ignorance has seriously added to the confusion. Science has for years contended that the Biblical chronology was not to be relied upon, and the Higher Critics some years ago showed that most of the older allegories show their Aryan origin and do not properly belong to Palestine, or to Jewish history, properly speaking, but the information raised such a hue and cry in the churches that the learned gentlemen who had advanced it subsided, without recanting, however, calmly waiting for the public mind to readjust itself to the changed view they had presented. Slowly but surely the ignorant bigot has retreated and intelligent understanding has advanced, until now few, even of the narrowest orthodox, hold to the chronology. In the last revision this ancient blunder was entirely discarded.

Fortunately for the cause of truth, the personal nouns and names of geographical locations have usually been left unchanged by the many translators during the ages, and in these words we find the key note of the most of the allegories when we can find their real meaning. In some cases the word is so ancient that the original meaning has been lost, but one can usually locate it to some degree by some little indication that throws light upon the subject. A child may take the notion that the book he studies had been written and published in the town in which he was born, not knowing that it could have been done anywhere else, but that does not interfere with his getting the lesson that its pages hold for him. Had Washington not lived, "Father of His Country" would not have any significance to us. These are the stories of the development of the great race to which we belong, not of one nation, and they really deal with things that happened, but just when they happened or just where they happened is not material; it is the lesson they hold for us that is important.

Intuition is one of the greatest of God's gifts to man, and it is one of the last of the faculties to develop, coming to its full growth only just before he finishes his compulsory earthly pilgrimages. These allegories are written in symbol to cultivate this wondrous gift and lead us to a complete at-one-ment with the Father. Consequently it is not surprising that at our stage of development we are only just beginning to sense the great riches lying just out of our reach. At best, at present, we are but catching glimpses of the sparkling treasures.

Occultists tell us that the great Manu, the Noah of our Bible, also the Moses, in one incarnation, began to select the most evolved of the great fourth root race, to start the new fifth root race during the fifth sub-race of the old race. In the Bible we find him also incarnated in Enoch (Initiator), begetting sons and daughters (spirtual sons and daughters in this reading), three hundred and sixty-five, note the number, the number of the days of the year, indicating that he worked to the full end of that race. The character of the Great One is indicated by the words, "And Enoch walked with God, and he was not for God took him." He was perfected in his Godhood, evidently a manifestation of a great perfected Soul. None of our own humanity had at that time attained that exalted position.

At the beginning of the sixth sub-race he appears as Noah, "And Noah walked with God." He was a righteous man and perfect in his generations, not generation, but generations; that is, perfect through many, many lives.

He begets, or gathers about him, three distinct classes of peoples symbolized by Shem (the name), those of a spiritual nature; Japheth (the more evolved of the race upon the Physical Plane); and Ham (the remnant of the other races who are just sufficiently interested, probably for personal gain, to follow the others).

In giving the allegorical reading, remember we in no way assail the fact of the occurrences having taken place; in fact, had they not taken place they would have been worthless for this symbolic use. Had Napoleon not fought, a man's meeting "his Waterloo" would mean nothing to us, and we would not use the expression; and so with these stories. When they were compiled probably they were illuminative because still comparatively fresh in the minds of the people either from legend, story, or experience, and to the Initiated explained the subjects satisfactorily.

Let us consider for a moment what information from the Orient tells us of the home of the great fourth root race. We are told that they lived upon a continent now under the sea that formerly occupied the place now taken by the Atlantic Ocean; that they lived and thrived for many ages; that the race being in its childhood was lead by numerous Great Ones from the planet Venus, where evolution is much more advanced than it is here, and that under this guidance they attained a great state of civilization. But the time came when the great teachers were withdrawn, all except the great Manu, the Regent of the Great Moon Chain, and man was left to his own devices to gain the experience of governing himself and his own affairs.

This was the time when the sons of God, or the descendants of Seth, went in unto the daughters of men, or the daughters of the third root race, those descended from Cain, probably the Lemurian race.

The Bible says "there were giants in those days, which were mighty men of old," and the Occultists tell us that the Lemurians were as tall as twenty-seven feet, and that the Atlanteans were also very large. The Lemurians were dark colored, but the Atlanteans were white. A Hindoo book says that man became black because of sin.

The fifth sub-race, from which Noah (Enoch) selected his people, was the one spoken of as Semitic, from the name Shem, to whom the Jews always pointed as their ancestor, and so he was, but no less was he the ancestor of us all. Shem had the double significance of referring to both a man and to his followers, and without doubt meant the Christ of the race, from the significance of the name. "The name" could refer to no one else. Noah, the great Manu, or lawgiver, and Shem, the Christ, together are shown leading the race to higher ideals. Shem is pictured as the son of the Manu, he always follows the Manu. The Manu gives the race the law and teaches them to be moral, then the Christ influence begins to slowly awake in them the higher ideals.

Noah preached the way of righteousness, we are told, for five hundred years during the fifth sub-race as Enoch, but the people would not listen; then he takes his followers and leads them to the Ark.

All tribes upon the face of the globe have a tradition of the flood,—a fine thing for an allegory, a historical fact that all understood and could be read literally, conveying a good moral lesson, but was suitable to convey a hidden spiritual meaning of much greater significance.

All of these names have a collective as well as an individual meaning. Noah means rest, peace harmony, harmony with God, a state of consciousness, as well as the name of an individual, even as Christ is a state of consciousness as well as the name of our Great Brother. Theosophy says Noah was the Seed Manu, or seed fifth root race Manu. He was Vaivasvata Manu. He was an understudy of Lord IHVH, He was the great over Lord of the race in one sense, looking after their physical development; in another sense He was the animating spirit of the race, the race itself; and in still another sense He was a perfect manifestation of the possibilities of the race. So much is hidden in this one word.

In one sense Noah, the Great Hierophant, preached righteousness to the people of Atlantis, and those who believed in him segregated in the course of the ages in the north country, under the Pole Star, the "Imperishable Sacred Land" it is called in Theosophic literature. This took place, we are told, about one million years ago. The Occultists agree with science in the tremendous length of time covered by the terse account given in the Biblical records. Not that they agree exactly as to the number of years, but both see the necessity for the assumption of many ages to accomplish the results.

About eight hundred and fifty thousand years ago, Noah led them southward to Aryavarta, from whence they scattered in the course of ages. Science finds them in this neighborhood; that is, finds ancient remains that indicate the fact that they were there.

"Ark" seems to have many meanings. The womb is sometimes called an ark, in the sense of containing and protecting the life germ. Baby Moses is represented as being placed in an ark of bulrushes. The Ark of the Covenant was a box containing the law of God, and in this allegory a great ship is pictured. It would seem that the general meaning of a place for safe keeping of valuables might cover the ground perhaps better than any other.

Let us look at this symbol a moment, and see if it really is a ship that is meant. May it not refer to the Imperishable North Land? First, the account says that the Land was filled with violence; the Hindoo accounts say that the strife between the black art and the Great White Lodge grew very fierce, and that the White Brothers and their followers were driven to the North Land while the Black Brotherhood completely took possession of the southern portion of the country.

Noah is told to build the ark of gopher wood. The Smith and Peloubet "Bible Dictionary" says that gopher wood in the Bible means "any trees of the resinous kind," so let us say it meant to find a safe place among the pines and fir trees of the north, a high-lying land. The ark was to have three rooms on each floor, even as man has three manifestations of God upon each plane, and it was to have three stories, even as man has three planes of consciousness. It shall be three hundred cubits in length, or three sub-races shall be the length of their stay, during the sixth and seventh sub-race of the fourth root race, and during one sub-race of the great fifth that is being born. In breadth it shall be fifty cubits, symbolic of the cultivation of the fifth race type. So the dimensions indicate the length of their stay, the characteristics they are to develop, and the three planes of the consciousness of the race. A "light" shalt thou make; the margin says a "roof." Strange that these two meanings should have been deemed a window. No other windows are mentioned. Would it not seem more probable that the "light" that could be read "roof" may mean establish a vibration by which the light of God may pour, sheltering the people from harm? A light and a shelter. A door there was; that is, there was communication between the two forces for awhile, but the day came when the Lord Jehovah sealed them up, and pitched the door; that is, put a stop to all communication between the two peoples. Those in the care of Noah were informed that there was danger for them in the low-lying lands, and they kept inside their ark, or their place of refuge, their highland home.

If we read the account literally, we must take it that Noah, Shem, Ham, and Japheth and their wives cruelly left their children to drown, but if it means that Noah was to take the three classes of people that had listened to him and their schools of wisdom, or their religious work, to another land, then the difficulty clears up.

He is to take the three classes of people who are represented as sons, and also seven or the perfect number of all clean animals, or some of each species, so they may not become extinct, and two, the creative dual, of the unclean animals. All sorts of living things must he take the pains to hold up in his northern region, for some of them being native to the low-lying lands would not stay unless forcibly detained. So Noah, the Great Manu whose duty it is to care for the physical well being of the race, took all these people, all these animals and creeping things into his ark, or his high-lying land under the Pole Star, and there he kept them while the great continent of Atlantis sank, and the ark, the land at the north, rose upon the face of the waters. As the continent went down the other land rose still higher. Ararat means high-lying land, or Holy ground, and the first thing Noah does is to build an altar, or establish a religion. The raven, the bird of ill-omen, is set loose and does not return, but the dove of peace returns and upon her second arrival carries an olive leaf, another symbol of the peace that is now established by the great cataclysm that has made all men brothers because of their common danger, and the great object lesson they have received of the danger that lies in rebellion against the powers of good.

Noah began his work of segregation in the fifth sub-race and is six hundred years old when the flood comes, or it is in the sixth sub-race that it comes.

NOAH AND THE FLOOD

Noah, upon establishing his religion, offers up burnt, or spiritual, offerings of all the things of the earth. He did not kill to do this; killing animals came long afterward, when men forgot the symbolic language and began to read these things literally.

God, in return, blesses Noah and tells him that man shall subdue all things, that every moving thing shall be meat, or shall supply your necessities, not to eat, because in the next clause of the same sentence we read, "the green herb have I given you all. But flesh with the life thereof which is the blood thereof shall ye not eat." Gen. ix, 3 and 4.

Then the covenant is entered into by God (symbolically, of course) that the race shall not be again destroyed by water. The Occultists tell us that water and fire take turns in bringing about the great race clean-ups and that the next will be by fire.

With the descendants of the three sons we are told the whole earth overspread, Shem, in one sense the Christ of the race, in another sense the most spiritual of the people, and his wife, or their inner school of Mysteries; Japheth, the normal, well-developed people of the race, the Material Plane, intellectual class of people who also had a wife or Mystery work that was not so advanced as that of Shem, for the latter seem to have started the priesthood of the race. Ham also had a wife or something that represents to the lower class of humanity an inner or esoteric work. All of the ancient religions had this as a part of the regular work, although it was according to the plane of the people how advanced the work would be. Ham means hot, or lustful, and the Hindoo scriptures say that man turned black because of sin. Evidently Ham was the remnant of the ancient races of different kinds that were not as evolved as the race called Japheth. They have no spiritual understanding, to speak of, for they laugh at Noah when he is presented to their eyes in spiritual ecstasy (or drunkenness).

Chapter ix, 20 of Genesis begins an allegory that brings another conception of Noah, a deeper and more mysterious meaning Here it is not the man Noah that is represented in one sense of the allegory, and in another sense it is. Noah began to raise grapes, the fruit of the Spirit, and became drunken in his tabernacle, and was uncovered, or naked. Ham saw and told his brothers, looked unabashed by the sight because of lack of finer feelings.

AN ESOTERIC READING OF BIBLICAL SYMBOLISM

In one sense the Great Hierophant, intent on spiritual things, in spiritual ecstasy, naked of possessions, is supplied by Shem the priesthood, and Japheth the people, walking backward, or unostentatiously, while the lower class people deride; but the other meaning shows another conception.

In the light of H. P. B., who defines Noah in one sense as the "seed of the fifth root race, the seed Manu, or man; Webster says: "The seed is the embryo and its envelope, or envelopes, that from which the plant grows." So Noah, the Great Guardian of the race, is cultivating spirituality in the race (growing vineyards), and the seed Manu is naked in its tabernacle, the germ of the new race is not yet clothed about with the vehicles that it is to use, but Shem cultivates the Soul, or mental body, and Japheth furnishes the astral and physical body without seeing what they are doing (going backward). The physical is God's back. Ham has no conception of what is going on. The symbolic curse is simply a prophecy:

"Cursed," or tied by the karma of his lack of development, will he be. "A servant of servants shall he be unto his brethren," while "Blessed be IHVH the God of Shem" (the God within. which is building up the soul of Shem).

"Canaan" (or Ham) "shall be their servant."

"God enlarge Japheth and let him dwell in the tents of Shem," that is, come into the spiritual consciousness of Shem.

And let Canaan, in one sense the lower nature, be servant of both of the higher planes of development.

And Noah lived after the flood three hundred and fifty years, or he kept in physical touch with the race three and one-half sub-races. The flood took place in the sixth sub-race and he stayed with them through the sixth, seventh, and the first of the fifth root race, until half of the second sub-race had passed, when he withdraws for a time from their physical sight.

Let us quote from "The Pedigree of Man," page 138: "About a million years ago Vaivasvata Manu chose out of the fifth Atlantean sub-race the Semitic, the seeds of the fifth race, and led them to the Imperishable Sacred Land. For ages he labors shaping the nucleus of future humanity. There the fifth sense is added and man is shaped as we know him. Thither he guides for rebirth the Asuras, to nobler ends. Thither he calls the brightest intelligences, the purest characters, to take birth in the forms he is evolving. When he had established the type of his race, he led them southward to Central Asia, and there another age-long halt was made 'from which in the course of ages several streams issued. Of these emigrations we will speak in another chapter.' "

CHAPTER VII.

THE SIGNIFICANCE OF THE TWO COVENANTS OF ABRAHAM.

Let us look at the two covenants of Abram and see what we find in the symbolic reading. Remember we do not for one moment assume that Abram was not a real personage, for we know that he was, and believe that in him we identify the Master Moro that to the Theosophist means so much. But the allegories have spiritual meanings that bring out definite stages in the development of the race as well as the development of the individual of whom it was primarily written.

Noah (if we are right), being the great seed Manu of the fifth root race, and Abraham the coming Manu of the sixth root race, serving under his great leader, then the stories of Abram stand out with startling clearness.

The reader will remember that Abram has just returned from rescuing Lot from his captivity in the mountain. Undoubtedly from the meaning of the names used, this was a great religious struggle, and Lot had gone into retirement upon spiritual heights. The word is brought to Abram as he is dwelling with the "oaks," or strong teachers of "Mamre." Now note, he takes 318 men of his household,—318 is the number of Jesus, and indicates purification,—he takes as his allies Mamre (manly), Eschol (courage), Aner (youth). So he takes purity (318), manliness, courage and youth, and he divides his forces at night, or leaves his physical body and goes out in his astral body to Lot to plead for his return to the lower plane people. All through the ages we see the Manu in his love for the common people pleading for the great spiritual leaders not to hide themselves in monasteries, but to stay among the people for teachers. He prevails and brings Lot back to the cities. When the king of Sodom, or the Physical Plane, tries to reward him he uses a figure of speech that Roberts tells us is still commonly used in India today, which shows the locality from which the story is derived: "I will not take a thread or a shoe-latchet," or the price of a worn sandal thong. But he wants due reward given to youth, bravery and manliness, which is the real cause of the spiritual opportunity being given them.

On the way back he meets Melchizedek, "King of Righteousness," "Prince of Peace." The ancient Jews claimed that Melchizedek was a son of Shem. A reincarnation of a person is sometimes spoken of as a son. Undoubtedly Melchizedek was an incarnation of Shem, or of the Buddha, while he was serving as the Bodhisattva, or the Christ, of the fourth root race. Abraham offers tithes to this Great One, who is spoken of as being a High Priest forever, without beginning of life or end of days, and of whom it was spoken when it was said of our Christ, "He shall be an High Priest forever after the order of Melchizedek." Melchizedek blesses Abraham in the name of El Elion (God the Mighty One), and Abram speaks of his protector being the Lord Jehovah; that is, he is a Manu and he bows before the Christ.

While he is with the great teachers he has a vision in which the Lord Jehovah appears to him and promises him all the land, or all the physical world, for his seed, and the people to cover it. The reader will notice that at this covenant the slain bodies of animals are used to signify that it is a Physical Plane contract, and that his animal nature must be offered up to God, (Heiffer); his rebellious sins (goat); and work in harmony with the Christ (ram), the lamb that was slain from the foundation of the world; to transmute the lower nature into the higher spiritual, as symbolized by the turtle dove (IH, creative wisdom of higher planes); and pigeon (the symbol of creative energy of lower planes, VH.)

It is really a covenant to conquer his lower nature and assist man to reach the point where he will look to the Christ for assistance to reach the goal of victory over the flesh.

His heirs, or his great fellow laborer, or laborers, ultimately shall come from his line, Isaac (an incarnation or a type of Him who is afterwards known as Jesus), and Jacob (afterwards known as the Christ). Here is the Trinity of the Great Ones who are to assist humanity through its long journey on the way to its eternal destiny, the Manu of the sixth root race; Jesus, a type of the Masters (the help of Jehovah); and Christ the Bodhissattva (Messiah) of the fifth root race. At the time of this covenant the Great Manu of the fifth root race is in charge of things of the VH degree of work, and the Buddha is filling the office of the Christ in the H degree.

This prophecy is brought out in verse 13, "Know of a surety that thy seed shall be sojourners in a land that is not theirs"; that is, shall live in the land of the fifth root race for a time, for four hundred years, or through four sub-races, will the sixth root race be living among the fifth race people who will not understand or will afflict them, but they will come out of the fifth root race with great substance (great wisdom), "And in the fourth generation they shall come hither again." That is, the sixth root race will begin to differentiate from the fifth root race in the fifth sub-race, and they will stay among the fifth root race until the first sub-race of the sixth root race is completed, then that will bring them up to the point of development in the new race that you Abraham represent now. And a smoking furnace, symbolic of the physical, and a flaming torch, symbolic of the spiritual, passed between the pieces, consummating the covenant after the ancient fashion. Now comes another promise and another covenant; this time it is not the material things that Jehovah sees, but because of all that this covenant implies He foresees that the true inheritance of the seed of Abraham will be all the land, or planes of consciousness between the river of Egypt, or the river of wisdom on the Physical Plane, and the great and abounding river, the river Euphrates, the wisdom of the Buddhic Plane. In other words, they shall ultimately conquer all of the planes of consciousness. It is the destiny of the fifth root race to fully develop the mental faculties, destined for this round, but the sixth root race will develop the higher mental and Buddhic faculties.

Sarai (my princess) is yet in the bondage of the flesh, so of her handmaid Hagar is born Ishmael, the child of the flesh, destined not to be circumcised, or to begin purifying his vehicles till the race reaches puberty; but his time will also come, so that his hand will no longer be turned against every man and every man's hand against him, because his mother, or his race, at once starts for the well of wisdom in the wilderness of ignorance, and "Jehovah seeth, yea and Jehovah careth for them, and will truly bring them

THE SIGNIFICANCE OF THE TWO COVENANTS OF ABRAHAM

forth into the promised land in due season." (They will also be brought into full consciousness of all the planes in due time.)

Ishmael was born when Abraham was four-score, perfected quarternary, symbolic of the perfected physical, and six, symbolic of physical but balanced karma. But when he was ninety years old and nine, here the triplicities are suggested in the age, three threes, and three threes, suggesting complete development of the triune nature; at this time he has another vision. This time it is El Shaddai, the Almighty God, the God of the higher planes, who speaks. Abraham is old, therefore symbolically pure. He has conquered the animal propensities, and is here given a second Initiation, for he receives his new name. Abram becomes Abraham, and Sarai becomes Sarah. "Be thou perfect" is the command. The Great One will give him the "land of his sojourning," the land of Canaan, or the four planes of consciousness for his inheritance. His covenant is to be an everlasting covenant, and the sign of this covenant is not slain animals but circumcision, a sign of purification.

Abram exalted Father becomes Abraham the father of multitudes; Sarai becomes Sarah, free princess, a princess no longer bound by the physical, but free to bring forth the child of the Spirit, the happy, laughing Isaac; happy because of the prospect of the happy upward tendency of the race. He is happy because he can be of service to the race. He, the help of Jehovah, is to train the race to develop the purity of life that will enable them to give birth to the Christ Child in the cave of their hearts. Happy, laughing Isaac, ultimately to become the scapegoat of the race in the most literal manner. I am assuming, of course, that Isaac was an incarnation of the entity whom we call Jesus. To my mind this is plainly indicated by the fact that Abraham circumcised 318 men in his household, the number of Jesus. Isaac, Jesus is the Spiritual son of Abraham, and Jacob (Christ), of Jesus. The Manu, or Abraham, is the manifestation of IHVH in the flesh, in the VH department of work; Jesus develops the H, or the higher creative energy, or wisdom; and Christ brings the father I, God into the Trinity of Manifestations, making the perfect whole, IHVH, Jehovah, the perfected Christ, the Messiah. God limited Himself to manifest. In Christ he has conquered matter, and is God free from fetters if he choses to be. He sits upon the right hand of the Father Almighty.

Jehovah in Abraham, is willing to place his beloved Isaac upon the altar in perfect consecration, and Isaac carries the wood willingly, the material to make the fire of the Spirit on the Mount of Initiation that shall consume his own lower nature, not then understanding the sacrifice that will be required. Abraham, when asked by Isaac where was the lamb, said God would Himself provide the lamb, and then taking the boy he put him upon the altar; but the physical life was not to be taken at that time, so another lamb was provided, symbolizing the fact that the lamb that was slain from the beginning of the world, the IHVH, was again consecrated, and this time to the second stage of its development in the flesh. The Master Isaac (Jesus) is not to die, but is to live all through the ages for the assistance of the race, teaching them to provide pure vehicles to bring forth the Christ. "And he shall be satisfied: By the knowledge of himself shall My righteous servant justify many; and he shall bear their iniquities." (Not in the sense of relieving them of their responsibility, but in the sense of sympathizing and assisting when possible.) "Therefore will I divide him a portion with the great" (He will make him one of the Great Ones who manifest the Trinity of God in the flesh, for the assistance of the race); "and he shall divide the spoil" (or the fruit of such service) "with the strong" (with Lord Jehovah and Christ); "because he poured out his soul unto death" (held it here in the lower regions for the sake of the race), "and was numbered among the transgressors; yet he bare the sin of many, and made intercession for the transgressors." Isaiah VIII, 11, 12.

How true, how beautifully true this is when we read it right. How heavy a load the dear Lord Jesus has borne. Think of the Spanish Inquisition and all of the other atrocities that have been done in His name. All through the ages has He worked in this middle place in the great scheme, trying through the exoteric religion to guide man to the realization of his true destiny, the development of the IHVH life within him. May the Infinite One reward this child of the Spirit, this fruit of Abraham's last covenant, according to His marvelous deserts. We will handle this life more at length in another chapter.

CHAPTER VIII.

MOSES.

As one ponders upon the allegories dealing with Moses guiding the great Aryan race, one is impressed with the wonderful depth of mystic meaning hidden behind the symbols, meanings so rich, so full of significance that one scarcely knows where to begin, or what to select from the wealth of riches, to bring before the reader anything like a comprehensive idea of the whole, in the space at our disposal. At best we can hope to touch but the high places, and possibly to place in the hand of the reader the golden key that will open to him the doors concealing the vision splendid. Just in proportion as he purifies himself, and turns it with clean hands, with a heart full of holy aspiration, and a mind steadied by meditation, will the vision open before him. The writer makes no pretense of having gained more than a glimpse, but that glimpse has convinced her that nothing else can compare with the glory that is hidden from our gaze by our own impurity, and that no sacrifice is too great to secure a closer view of the wonders of the Temple of God.

Some remarkable symbols are used in these allegories, symbols as old as humanity itself. In a former chapter it was mentioned that IHVH were the symbols representing the Trinity of manifestations of God, and that these four letters are sometimes used to designate the Three Great Streams of creative activity as they flow; sometimes to designate one of the three Great Ones, the Lord Jehovah, He who looks after the first of the three stages of man's evolution, that signified by the letters VH; and sometimes used to designate the Spirit in the heart of man, as when Eve, the physical body of humanity, said, "I have gotten IHVH" (Jehovah), or, I am completed by IHVH.

As we have said before, the letters VH stand for a stage in the evolution of man. The incarnating Spirit, the Ego, descends through the elemental kingdoms of the Buddhic, Mental, and Astral planes of matter, and enters the human body. It is looked after during this stage by the great Lord Jehovah. The Hindoo calls this Great One the Manu, the ancient Hebrew called him also Noah and Moses. He is allegorically shown as guiding the race up to the time when man reaches the place where he says, "I am tired of the husks of desire, I will arise and go to my Father." The Lord Jehovah has assisted him to gain a perfect body in which to manifest, containing a brain of almost unlimited possibilities, and He has provided the child race with an environment that will develop this intellect that lies dormant, within him. We note that He ever tries to keep spiritual teachers among His young races, and also tries to make their experiences as little painful as possible to give the needed lessons. Remember how He pleads, as Moses, for the children of Israel when they sin. He provides them with a simple code of morals (if read literally, and the child race ever reads literally), that develops the moral nature and cultivates the intellect. At last, however, the day comes when the IHVH (the God), in the heart of man, ever crying for fuller expression, impels man to say "I will arise and go to my Father." Then it is that the Lord Jehovah, Manu, Moses lays his hands upon Joshua, Jesus, or whoever may happen to be serving in that department, the second stage of the development of man, symbolized by the letter H, signifying the creative love wisdom of the higher planes. The work of this stage is to train the man to build up a soul, or causal body, fit for the birth of the Christ Child in his heart, for the Christ is ever of immaculate conception, descending as a dove of peace from above, and vivifying the latent spiritual atoms of the inner IHVH, so they may become active.

The "I," the Hebrew letter "Yod," symbolizes the third stage in the development of man, and is represented to us in perfection of manifestation by the Great One whom we call the Christ. There was a day in our Scripture, however, when the entity whom we know as the Christ had not yet attained the exalted height that He now occupies, and His advance along the line of promotion is shown in some of the allegories.

As Jacob He had conquered with God, and received His new name; in the first of the Moses allegories we find Him incarnating as the brother of the Manu (Moses), and serving as priest Aaron, in the second, or H department of work. The two take Hebrew (Heber, passed over) parentage (or those who had passed over the line into the new fifth race) of the priestly caste (the tribe of Levi). River symbolizes wisdom, while Pharaoh is a symbol of power, or dominance, and the daughter of the king is a class of the inner or Mystery work of the time, a manifestation of the H, the creative love wisdom. The double meaning of the symbols is plainly seen here. Moses is an incarnation of the Great One come into the flesh to assist man in his development, but he is also just as truly a type of humanity in the development of the physical, mental and moral natures of the vehicle he occupies in that incarnation. The Kabbalah says Moses was perfect from his birth, and Theosophy says the Manu was perfected on the Moon Chain. This idea is brought out by the Kabbalah in the numerical significance of Moses, 345, or God's back; while God's face is 543, and the sum of God's back and God's face is 888, or the number of the Christ. This indicates that humanity and God perfectly harmonized makes a Christ; the perfect union of God and man. Spirit the positive pole, and matter the negative pole is perfectly balanced. All is God. "Hear, O Israel, the Lord our God is one God," says Moses; "There is no God but God," proclaims the Mohammedan; "The Lord, before and beyond whom there is no other," affirms the Zoroastrian; "One only, without a second," says the Hindoo; "In Him we live and move and have our being," says the Christian; "The Father and I are One," says the Christ. Many selves all fragments of the One Great Self, subhuman, human and superhuman, and therefore destined to perfection, and when that perfection is reached we shall have unity, Christ, 888.

Stop a moment and see how much is expressed by those three figures. The quaternary symbolizes the perfected physical, the Trinity the perfected God, and duality is a symbol of the Second Logos, so in these three figures we have the dual quaternary, repeated three times, the perfect Trinity, the perfect physical united in the Wisdom of the Second Manifestation of the Trinity.

We will keep in mind that the symbols have the double meaning of referring to the typical experiences of humanity, as well as of giving those of the entity incarnated in the body that we call Moses. It is significant that the Hindoo word signifying this individual is Manu, or man, and we have just shown that the

Hebrew Kabbalah shows this same conception by the number 345. For the sake of simplicity and because of lack of space we will handle Moses in the singular, leaving it to the reader to trace the similitude of the experiences of the Great One to that of the race in general.

Keep in mind that not only the man, but the fifth root race is meant by Israel or Jacob, Jacob the race unregenerate, Israel after the spiritual develops; Judah, symbolic of the Jews, Esau and Ishmael and their descendants the fourth and a half root races, the race between the old Atlanteans and the new fifth root race, and that any of them may be called Hebrews, or those who crossed over into the new race. Pharaoh stands for the dominance of the physical, and Egypt means the Physical Plane except when referring to Mystery work, then it stands for the home of the Great White Lodge. When "in bondage to Egypt," then the Physical Plane is meant, but when the party voluntarily "goes down into Egypt," then the White Lodge is sought.

Moses drawn out of the river of Wisdom by the orders of a daughter of Pharaoh, a class of Mystery work, comes to the point that he realizes the bondage of Egypt (or the flesh), and in trying to protect the Hebrew (develop the characteristics of the new race), he kills the Egyptian, or possibly conquers his lower nature. Such a radical step is not understood by those about him, and he is made to feel that his life (his spiritual life) is in danger if he remains among the crowd, so he betakes himself to a well of wisdom. Jethro, a priest of Midian, is this well of wisdom, who has just what Moses is after. He understands the sciences of the higher planes, which are called his "seven beautiful daughters." Moses studies with him and marries, or masters one of them so perfectly that he is given that part of the work to carry on himself, for we are told that he herded Jethro's sheep on the hillsides. He taught his people on the spiritual heights.

An ancient Hebrew book says that Jethro was an incarnation of the essential spirit of Abel, which shows the reverence in which this man was held, for name Abel means spirit, breath, and indicates the nature of the man who could be conceived as being an incarnation of him.

When on the mountain of spirituality, Moses hears the voice of "I AM THAT I AM" from a burning bush. As bush symbolizes a teacher, and as burning would indicate spirituality, it may mean that it was a great spiritual teacher through whom Moses received his call to service, although it is not at all necessary, for one so highly evolved as Moses could have communed personally with higher forces.

He is told to remove his shoes, as the ground whereon he stands is holy; the Oriental always removes his shoes before entering a temple, so this is a symbol of reverence. He is called to service of a new kind in Chapter 6-3, El Shaddai IHVH of higher planes, explains that he has hitherto appeared to the people only in his power aspect, exacting only their obedience to physical laws, but now the time has come for them to realize the fuller significance of Jehovah, and He is about to reveal His love and wisdom aspect. Heretofore the VH aspect has been in control, Spirit has been descending and gathering vehicles about Himself ready to manifest, but now the time has come for Spirit to start upon its homeward journey toward the GOD who sent it forth. Spirit ascending calls upon thee, Moses, to assist him to get out of the bondage of the flesh.

"But," says Moses, "how can I with uncircumcised lips do this thing?" This body is now thoroughly awake as to the great ego that it holds, and the great work he has been doing throughout the ages. How can I, who have worked in the physical vibration to enable Spirit descending to gather about itself proper vehicles in which to manifest? How can I do this other work that will tend to undo much that I have done? I have taught man to gather to himself material necessities; now he must be taught not to prize the very things for which he has trained himself to exert his greatest efforts. This new work belongs to the H, or love and wisdom department of the work. How can I do the two? So the Voice tells him to get his brother Aaron (an incarnation or type of the one we know as Christ), and he will attend to this part of the work,—but Moses is to show that the perfected physical recognizes that this is the natural destiny of man, and is to lead the race to a strong moral understanding that will help the priestly offices of Aaron to be effective.

Moses, we are told, was four-score years old, a perfected quaternary, or physical, and Aaron was four-score and three, a quaternary topped by the triangle, or the spiritual triad.

AN ESOTERIC READING OF BIBLICAL SYMBOLISM

Aaron, although he is the entity whom we call the Christ today, served in that incarnation in the capacity that Jesus is serving in today, that of teaching man to purify his vehicles and build up his soul preparatory to the birth of the Christ Child in his heart, or the First Great Initiation.

Moses starts to do as commanded, and here we have that incomprehensible passage, when read literally, in Ex. iv, 24, "And it came to pass on the way, at the lodging place, that Jehovah met him and sought to kill him." Then Zipporah took a flint and circumcised her son, so He let him alone. Strange, very strange, that God should seek to kill one who is starting to do just as he has been directed to do; surely none will gainsay that this must be an allegory hiding some esoteric secret.

But if we accept Zipporah as a method of scientific instruction in unfoldment, according to old-time Mystery work methods, then the two sons begotten by her would simply be students, or Initiates. Let us look at the meaning of the words a moment. Zipporah—"little bird,"—a bird is a symbol of the creative energy of the Trinity: "Gershom,"—we find that the Gershomites were the priestly family descended from the son of Levi.

Now remember that Moses sat himself down by the well of wisdom, and the seven daughters (called the Shining Ones in some ancient books) came to draw, to water their father's flock, or they came to give of the water of wisdom to the people. There were other teachers who opposed their system, but Moses upheld them. Some esotericists claim that Jethro's daughters were the seven sciences, some that they were the science of mastering the seven planes. At any rate, they referred to learning of some kind, undoubtedly. So this passage in the fourth chapter, 24 to the 27th verses, may easily mean that when Moses started to do God's bidding, the Jehovah within himself said to him, I will kill your lower nature, and he struggled to have that done, and, at the same time, taught Gershom, or the priestly class of the people, the science of purification according to the system of Zipporah. Circumcision was always a symbol of purification.

"A bridegroom of blood art thou because of the circumcision," she is represented as saying; that is, thou shalt bring the people, humanity, people of blood, Physical Plane people, up to the point of purification. Thou art a bridegroom of humanity upon the

Physical Plane. Thou art married to humanity until their purification is accomplished.

That the two sons were spiritual sons is admitted by many, from the fact that they disappear from the genealogical records, and no further mention is made of them in Scripture as Moses' sons. At his death it is Joshua, and Eleazar, Jesus and Master K. H. who go up into the mountain with him. Aaron has passed from earthly view just before, and Zipporah is never mentioned after Jethro comes to visit Moses, and they take communion together.

The episode of circumcision takes place just before he goes up on the Mount of God to meet Aaron, surely a fitting time to let the God within get complete mastery, a fitting struggle to enable him to mount the spiritual height that may be called the Mount of God.

Moses and Aaron meet in love with kisses, and both proceed together to go down into Egypt, or to the Physical Plane people, to teach them the lessons they are sent to teach.

Pharaoh, or the dominant physical tendencies of the race, scorns the message at first, and only as the miracles, one by one, show them the danger of the course they are pursuing, are they convinced and realize the necessity of going a three-day journey to worship God, or taking the three stages of purification, the purification of body, of desire body, and of mental body, to build up a soul in which the Christ Child can manifest.

All of the miracles teach the same lesson, that if the creative energy that is pouring through them be used in blessing to others then it will create in blessing to the race, but man is a free will being and can poison the stream at its source if he so chooses, and can transmute this great creative force into a curse. It is the nature of this force to create, but it lies with him whether the portion allotted him shall flow out in constructive creation, or whether it shall become a destructive force bringing forth all sorts of pests to torment mankind, causing all sorts of disease bacteria, and all sorts of inharmonies in nature that bring pain upon man. This force flows out in whatever work we do. The motive decides the result.

Let us take a hasty glance at the miracles. It is a tempting place to linger, but we must not take too much space.

Serpents, the reader will remember, have always been used as a symbol of wisdom, and the word is often a symbol of a wise teacher. Aaron's serpents swallow those of the wise men; that is, the wisdom of Aaron comprehends all that the materialistic teachers can set forth, and has so much more that the materialistic arguments are lost.

Rivers are symbolic of wisdom; rivers turned into blood, wisdom defiled by the blood of innocent animals, when true wisdom calls for the sacrifice of the animal nature of man upon the altar of devotion.

The emanations of man sent out with selfishness as his controlling motive brings forth pests (lice) that because of the nature he has given them, feed upon him, destroying his peace. Flies are also symbolic of the offspring of filthy habits. Even the poor animals will suffer from the bacteria (murrain) brought into existence by the selfish disregard of God's law that unregenerate man indulges in.

Death of the first born, shows that the creative energy must create, but if it be poisoned by selfish motives, then it turns inward, instead of flowing outward, in all sorts of creative activities that bless others; and being so strongly creative it creates destructive agents in his own system that tend to destroy him. Thus the eldest born of Egypt, those who will not turn from the selfish course, will die; while the first born of Israel, the spiritual minded of the race who are willing to sprinkle the blood, or the life of the Christ, the Lamb that was slain from the beginning of the world, upon the lintel of the doorposts of their hearts, will be saved alive. Thus does the IHVH in the heart of each work out his blessing or his curse. And this is the only sense in which God ever curses his children. The God in man's own heart, in trying to manifest, is sometimes forced to let his creative force destroy the form that binds him down, and will not let him manifest his Godlike nature.

A little touch of occult knowledge is given us in Ex. 8, 20: Moses rises up early to remonstrate with Pharaoh. It's in our first moments after waking that our higher selves can most often make themselves heard, while we are passive, and our senses are all quiet, then can the still small voice be heard.

The rod used was the rod of Initiation, and as a rule it is

Aaron who wields it, in this case, though Moses takes it when he needs the assistance of the water elementals to bring forth hail, symbolic of hardened physical desire, which will beat down all the natural fruits of the world, leaving all things desolate and forbidding. Thus did the great Law Giver and the High Priest train the people to understand the necessity of building up a soul, a fit vehicle for the Christ to manifest in. Thus did these two Great Ones work together in perfect harmony, nay, three Great Ones and more worked together in harmony, for the three great lines of work were carried on by those whose duty it was to look after them.

The Great Trinity of helpers of mankind at one time stood: First, the Lord Jehovah; second, the one whom we know as the Christ; and, third, Melchizedek, or the Buddha. Today it stands: Lord Jehovah, Jesus, and the Masters of whom He is a type, and the Christ, in the departments respectively of VH. of H, and of I, or Yod; thus is the work of the Holy Ghost, the Son, and the Father carried on by these Great Ones who are each a perfect Manifestation of all three Outpourings of the Supreme.

Perhaps Jesus has been allowed to be more prominent than the rest of the Masters who may be found working right with Him everywhere in the Bible, because to Him was given the care of the religion of the western branch of the great Aryan race.

If any doubt my right to call Moses a perfect manifestation of the IHVH in the Trinity of Great Ones, I refer him to Ex. 7, 1: "And IHVH said unto Moses, I have made thee as a God to Pharaoh, and Aaron shall be thy prophet." Later on when he initiates Joshua, and also strikes the rock of the Master of Compassion twice for Aaron and Eleazar which brings forth the stream of wisdom that waters not only the Children of Israel, the Spiritual people, but also the cattle or the common people. He acts as Great Initiator.

Because he has done this he cannot go into the Promised Land with the people for the reason that he is already there, and he lays his hands upon Joshua (Jesus) and turns the people over to him, that he may guide them through the descending torrent (Jordan) of the degenerative tendencies of the race. When Joshua starts to take the race through this descending torrent of their desires what does he do? He places the Ark of the Covenant, that symbol of the Christ Man, where it will stay the flood, and so long as that symbol is placed in a prominent place before the people the waters are kept back. Crossing through the bed of the river, twelve rocks (Masters of Compassion) are picked up, or developed by the struggle, and twelve more are found on the other side, just as they came up out of the river. So here are twenty-four Masters of Compassion given in the Bible as being the result of this struggle against the tide of desire.

Before this Moses had gone up into the Mount of God, and he got revelations he could not give to the people because they were not ready, so he established Mystery work and transmitted the Spoken Law to Joshua, who in turn gave it to the forty receivers or elders, and these in turn communicated the same to those who qualified themselves to receive it.

All through the ages has this been done, but after the destruction of the second temple an effort was made to embody this teaching in a set of allegories that should hide while yet telling these truths to the initiated eye. We call this book the "Kabbalah." It is doubtful if we yet perceive more than a fraction of the meaning hidden there.

So we see these Moses stories are telling us the occult secrets by which we may conquer flesh, and also reveal to us the great fact that loving elder brothers are standing ever ready to assist the race, no matter at what altitude the individual may stand; loving hands are ever ready to assist him, loving hearts ever ready to sympathize with him. The Passover we see is not only a Jewish historical point, but is a point of universal significance, being no less a place than the point when the spirit has definitely and consciously conquered the flesh up to the point of turning its back upon the downward course, and turning its face consciously to the Father who sent it.

CHAPTER IX.

REINCARNATION IN THE BIBLE.

Reincarnation is a doctrine little understood in western lands. To the average Christian it means a belief in the return of the human soul into the forms of animals or some of the lower kingdoms. This, however, is not the sense in which it is used by Occultists today.

It is recognized that such things as obsessions do occur sometimes, just as monstrosities are sometimes born, but such cases are abnormal. The tide of evolution is ever onward and upward. It is not God's law that a decent animal should be polluted by a degenerate human entity.

Science has traced the evolution of the human body up through the lower kingdoms, but, as Mrs. Besant has said, they have not given us the evolution of man when they have given us the evolution of the body, because the body is not the man, it is only the dress he wears; there must also be the evolution of the intellect, and of the soul, before the evolution of man can be said to have been given; this the doctrine of reincarnation supplies.

Reincarnation is found in all of the older religions, the Hebrew and early Christian included, as any one can prove who will take the pains to read the writings of the early Church Fathers. The foolish notions begotten in ignorance, to be found among the lower classes of the Orient today naturally repel the American or the Englishman, but if one will but seek the underlying truth he will at once see the reasonableness of the assumption.

Many of the clergy are today convinced of the truth of this doctrine, but not many dare to state it plainly because of the intolerance of their people. For that reason the writer refrains from quoting many hints that have been dropped by noted clericals that indicate their broad views along these lines. It is unnecessary to make trouble for others to prove our argument.

Science has demonstrated that according to the age he is destined to live, will be the time that it takes an animal to reach maturity. The insect reaches full maturity in an hour, and dies in a day; the dog is full grown in a year, and lives a dozen years or more; the horse matures in three or four years and lives twenty-five or thirty years; the elephant takes many years to mature and lives hundreds of years; so, also, man's physical body falls into line, and uses a proportionate time to prepare for its earthly existence. The law seems to be uniform, and, as above so below; therefore, may we not reason that the soul or mental body must have an opportunity to build the body for the Eternal Spirit to manifest in commensurate with the age to which it is expected to live?

The soul cannot be said to be really immortal, that is, the mental body, for that is what the Hebrew meant by the soul when he spoke of body, soul, and Spirit, and will in time slip off to allow the Spirit to mount higher than it can follow, but so long as the Spirit needs it to manifest in upon the lower planes, it will survive, and that to us, in our present state of evolution, is practically immortality. If this one life is all that we have to look forward to, and if all of our eternal future depends upon the use we make of this one life, then we are "of all men most miserable," for, with the most of us, about all that we really accomplish is to gain a realization of how far we fall short of the ideal, nor can we see anyone whom we can feel at all sure, has attained to the desired point of perfection.

How can God be proven to be just, allowing, as He does, children to be born under all sorts of varying conditions in all sorts of places, with all sorts of parents, if He then stipulates that all must believe exactly the same things or be lost? If one life is all there is, the thing is impossible; but if the child in the slums is there because in some other life he caused others to suffer that very same trouble, and needs to find out how it feels to be treated that way, then one can see the justice of the dealing. If each life is a day in school, and if all have the chance to ultimately pass, if they will but do their part, there is a satisfaction in contemplating the scheme. The grandeur of it grows upon one as he studies it, and a new feeling of brotherhood grows up in one's heart.

REINCARNATION IN THE BIBLE

Christ showed that He understood the doctrine and did not condemn it, when he asked Peter who men said that He was? Peter said, Some say Elias, and some say some of the other prophets. But who do you say that I am? Luke ix, 13, 20; Mark viii, 27, 29. "And Peter answering said unto Him, Thou art the Messiah."

"When talking of John, He said plainly: "This is Elijah, that was to come; he that hath ears to hear let him hear." Matt. xiv, 13, 16 and xvii, 10, 13. That is, those who understand the Mysteries will understand this matter, but He cautions the disciples not to speak of it.

So also is the case of the blind man when the question was asked, "Did this man sin or his parents?" for of course a man born blind could not have sinned before his birth, unless he had lived before. Had the question been foolish He would not have answered as He did, but He seems to have recognized the justice of the question, and explains that in that case neither had sinned. John ix, 1, 3.

In James iii, 6, we read of the "wheel of birth," some of the versions make it read the "wheel of nature," but one will usually find "birth" in the margin, when it is put that way.

The resurrection of the body, to suffer the penalty of the sins done in the body, as given in the Christian creed, no doubt refers to this understanding, as it was held in the early church.

Our only object in stating these things is to prepare the mind to see the indications of the proof of this docerine in the allegories as we proceed. Let us see if we can not identify some of the incarnations of the Great Ones that we know best, in these ancient stories.

The writer makes no claim to be able to read the akasic records, and if any one has done so to seek for these lives, she is ignorant of the fact; but she feels impressed with the conviction that she has discovered some incarnations that will stand the test of occult investigation, and perhaps a good many. At any rate, it is interesting to study the indications, whether they be the real incarnations or be used simply as types for our instruction.

We are told that a Great Soul who has incarnated many times to assist mankind, is called by the Hindoos the "Manu," and that in the fifth sub-race of the fourth root race he started to gather the most advanced of the race to start the new fifth root race (the Aryan race). In our Bible we find in Genesis, Lord Jehovah given, and Noah, a "man righteous and perfect in his generation, who walked with God." In Moses, we find a great Law Giver like the Manu of the Hindoo, in Enoch (Initiator) one "who walked with God and was not for God took him" (or who was buried in the inner Mystery work of the time); in Samuel, another Initiator, or anointer, and in Zerrubbable also a great Initiator, his name means one who was born at the gate of God, or at the gate of Initiation. If there is anything in reincarnation then these names have a deeper significance than is apparent from casual reading. May they not all be incarnations of the Manu or his assistants?

In Shem, in Melchizedek, and in Jonathan there are many indications that remind one of the Buddha.

In Israel, in Aaron, in Samson, and in David we may see our blessed Master Christ. "I am the root (Israel), and the offspring (in Jesus' body) of David, his bright and morning star." (The first of the race to show the star of Initiation.)

"Thus saith Jehovah, if My covenant of night and day stand not, if I have not appointed the ordinances of heaven and earth; then will I also cast away the seed of Jacob, and of David my servant (note, my servant, not my servants), so that I will not take his seed (again the singular, evidently one person is referred to as "Jacob" and "David") to be rulers over the seed of Abraham, Isaac, and Jacob."

Let us see if we cannot find Jesus in his other incarnations as mentioned in the Bible, as Isaac, as Joshua with Moses, as Joshua the High Priest of Beth Shemish, and as Joshua the High Priest in Zach. III, 6, 19: "In those days, and at that time I will cause a branch of righteousness to grow up unto David; and he shall execute justice and righteousness in the land. Jer. 23, 5. A branch to grow up from the Lord Jehovah to David, who fits in here like Jesus, whose name means Jehovah's helper, growing up to David, forming a branch with the Christ?

We are told by Occultists that our Christ is to be succeeded by the Master K. H., who is to act as the Christ of the sixth root race even as Christ succeeded the Buddha. Let us see if we find Master K. H. in Lot, in Joseph, in Eleazar, in Solomon, and in John the Beloved?

They tell us also that Master Moro is to be the Manu, or Law Giver of the sixth root race and that he has been an understudy of the Great Manu for ages; let us see if we can find him in the lives of Abraham, in Elijah, in John the Baptist.

Let us look at Baalim and Jonah and see if we can find Peter, dear, loving-hearted, impulsive Peter, always doing the impulsive thing, yet whom Christ addressed as "famous son of spirit," taking "dove" as a symbol of spirit, prophesying that he would become a stone (or a Master) in that incarnation. We are told that he was crucified, in legend.

Such conjectures are important only as showing that the doctrine is taught in the book that has been claimed as contradicting it. Akasic investigation may prove that we have made some mistakes, but it will also prove that we have in many instances been right; of this the writer feels convinced.

This doctrine, and the accompanying one, that of cause and effect, or compensation, "Karma" the Hindoo would say, "Be not deceived; God is not mocked, whatsoever a man soweth that shall he also reap"; these two ensure perfect justice to the son of man and the possibility of attaining ultimate perfection, even as the Master commanded, "Be ye therefore perfect even as your Father in heaven is perfect." Upon this plane if a man sows corn in Kansas, he does not expect to reap beans in Missouri; so, neither may he, if he sows agony and bloodshed in this body, reap fire in a body that will not feel the flames. He must come back here and suffer the very pain he inflicted. Thus will the will of God be done, that we become perfect through experience, and we suffer only what we bring upon ourselves. "It is not My will that one of these little ones should perish." Not one jot or one tittle of the law shall fail, till all things be accomplished." Matt. v, 18.

CHAPTER X.

CAN JESUS BE IDENTIFIED IN OTHER LIVES?

The thought of reincarnation is so new to the western world, that to the average mind it will require a distinct struggle to readjust the ideas that have controlled the thought for years; and this is not an easy thing to face. But do not be frightened, friends; nothing that you or I can do will in any way disturb the Eternal Verities, but we may by patient endeavour obtain a better and truer understanding, and thus gain unspeakably.

In considering the incarnations of Jesus, the first that the writer identifies with the Blessed Elder Brother, is that of Isaac, the spiritual son of Abraham (Master Moro, the understudy of the great Manu, or Lord Jehovah).

Abram has become Abraham, or has taken the Second Great Initiation, before this child of the Spirit is born. "For it is written that Abraham had two sons, one by the handmaid, and one by the free woman. Howbeit, the son by the handmaid is born of the flesh; but the son of the free woman is born through promise, which things contain an allegory; for these women are two covenants; one from Mount Sinai, bearing children unto bondage, which is Hagar." Gal. IV, 23 and 24. Then in the 28th verse Paul says: "Now we brethren, as Isaac was, are children of the promise." 29: "But as then he that was born after the flesh, persecuted him that was born after the Spirit; so now", etc.

In this passage Paul supports me in the assumption that physical women and physical children are not figuring in the allegories, but are used as symbols of spiritual things.

The spiritual child, Isaac, is dedicated to the service of God from the first, and willingly goes with his father up into the mount (of Initiation), carrying the fuel for his own sacrifice, or the spirit of love and devotion, although he was at yet ignorant of the full significance of the act, as is shown by his questions. He makes no resistence when Abraham places him upon the altar, although the idea seems to be that he thought that death was the necessary outcome of the service. But God shows him that his work will consist in living all through the ages to help man, not in dropping the body, but in retaining it. The peculiarly gentle, devoted, loving nature of Isaac has often been spoken of by Bible students.

When he is forty (the perfected quaternary, symbolic of the perfected physical), his father causes to be brought to him especial teaching in the Mystery work of Laban the Great White Brother, which is symbolized by Rebecca. As soon as he sees the beautiful higher Wisdom he loves it, and is at once married to it, or makes it one with him. It is significant that Isaac first sees Rebecca when in the field, *meditating*.

There are those who claim that this is one of the incarnations of the one whom we call the Christ, but as Christ Himself speaks of Jacob and Isaac as two distinct entities in the words "God is the God of Abraham, Isaac, and Jacob, God is the God of the living, not of the dead," and as we feel sure that Jacob was an incarnation of the Christ, and as Jesus seems to have ever worked in the degree between the Lord Jehovah, and the Christ, making a Trinity of Great Ones, that we distinguish at every turn in the affairs of humanity, it looks probable that we are right

In the next incarnation of this Great Soul, however, it is easier to see the distinguishing characteristics by which we know Him. We will first look at the meanings of the names, and see what we find:

In the Smith and Peloubet "Bible Dictionary" we find the meaning of Jesus given as "The Greek form of the name 'Joshua,' or 'Jeshua,' a contraction of 'Jehoshua'; that is, help of Jehovah, or Saviour." Right here is stated that he is the "help of the Lord Jehovah," as we have pointed out. At the mention of Joshua the mind at once reverts to the minister of Moses. Now we are told by those who have the ability to judge correctly, that Moses was a manifestation of the Great Law Giver, or the "Manu" of the fifth root race. It must have meant much to be in such close touch with the Great Manu. It rather startles one to note that Joshua is called the son of "Nun," when we find that

"Nun" means "Fish," and we are reminded that the astrological sign of Jesus was Pisces, and that the early Christians used this sign as a kind of token to distinguish each other when among enemies.

We must remember that Moses is the leader of all of the Aryan race, not of the Jews only. "Judah" refers to the Jews, "Israel" to the whole Aryan race, in symbolic language, with its twelve, or perfect number of nations. And Moses turns the guidance of the race over to Joshua, when they reach the Jordan, symbol of the degenerative tendencies of the strongly developed desire nature. His the work of teaching this people the lessons of self control and purity.

In Numbers XI:28, we find Joshua spoken of as minister of Moses from his youth up; this may, of course, mean for only that life, but "youth" may mean his Isaac incarnation.

Joshua is one of Moses' "chosen men." In Numbers XIII, we find he is one of twelve, chosen by Moses to go to spy out the Promised Land (or the planes of extended consciousness). In another chapter the reader will see a description of the Garden of Eden, where the Promised Land is shown to be the planes of consciousness, from the land of Cush, or the Physical Plane, to the full and abounding River of Wisdom (Euphrates) on the Buddhic, Universal Love Plane. So Moses chooses twelve of his best men, to start esoteric work, to learn under his direction how to develop the powers latent in man, that would enable them to function consciously upon the higher planes of consciousness, the "Promised Land," the ultimate destiny of the race.

Up to this time the young man had been called "Hoshea," in that incarnation, but now Moses gives him the name of "Joshua," or gives him the Second Great Initiation. As Isaac, he had shown his willingness to place himself upon the altar at the call of Abraham, and had gone up into the Mount of Initiation, carrying the fuel of the sacrifice in his own hands, or having in himself the consecration to feed the flame of the spirit. There, he took the First Great Initiation, here he takes the second, and receives his new name. In Ex. XXIV, 13, we find that Joshua, alone, went up into the mount (of Initiation) "with Moses." Ten of the men who had been chosen became discouraged, or died metaphorically; it was too big an undertaking to conquer the desire nature sufficiently to enter the land of the higher planes, and the spiritual impulse dies. Only Joshua and Caleb are left alive upon the higher altitudes, and only Joshua goes up into the mount with Moses (is initiated).

Mr. Leadbeater says, that a man may be called at any time by sounding the name of the Augoeides, for that is the chord of the three principles of the Ego, and the Monad behind, so no matter where the man may be, when that chord is sounded his causal body (his soul) lights up, and leaps upward like a great flame, plainly visible to the seer. Page 140, "Inner Life," Vol. II. This is evidently the "new name" given in the Bible at the Second Great Initiation, and I think I am right in saying, that this name or one of the same rhythmic value, will be found identifying the Ego in succeeding incarnations. In the case of Jesus, the name of Joshua, the Hebrew for Jesus, is consistently used throughout the allegories where he is mentioned. This makes it easier than it proves to be with the Christ, who has such a number of names. But we will handle that later.

Let us see where we find Joshua figuring in the Old Testament:

In I Sam. vi, 14, we find Joshua a high priest in the temple of the Sun God, at Beth-Shemish, or the ancient Heliopolis, of Egypt. The Philistines, the descendants of Esau, the fourth and a half root race, strongly Physical Plane people, had taken the Ark of the Covenant from Israel in battle, but did not know what to do with it.

The Ark, the reader will remember, symbolized the ideal of the fifth race man, the perfect, the God Man, the destiny of the fifth root race, and understandable by them, but the Philistines were simply disturbed by the suggestion. Perfection was beyond their conceptions; so they placed the Ark in the temple with their god Dagon, a symbol of the Astral Plane, half fish half man. The poor old god of the desire nature at once recognized that its conqueror had come, and fell upon his face, and when set up again he broke himself in pieces in his effort to humble himself. This made the Philistines so uncomfortable that they decided to get rid of this disagreeable reminder of man's destiny.

Let us look at the beauty of the symbols used: First, the "Ark of the Covenant" made of Shittim, or the imperishable wood of the Orient, overlaid inside and outside with the gold of God's righteousness and wisdom, with the law of God in the heart of it, containing also the pot of mana (manas, mind), symbol of the intellect, or rather the higher mind, for it came from above, overshadowed by the Cherubim, and continually receiving a stream of power from God,—the perfect man, the Christ. Naturally the poor physical-natured descendent of Esau would be far more comfortable with Dagon, the god of desire. Now note the other symbols. They took two "kine," confining their calves. Does not the reader see the symbol? Creative animal nature leaving its young, or all material attractions, even those most deeply rooted in the heart. They are "turned loose upon the highway," hitched to a cart containing the Ark, to go as they may choose. When the ideal of the race is really loaded upon the animal nature what happens? It forgets every material consideration and they start at a brisk pace, lowing with longing as they go, toward the temple of the sun (or God) "at Beth Shemish, in to the field" (the immortal life field) of Joshua the High Priest, and stand by a "stone" (the rock of our salvation), and upon this "Stone" is placed the Ark, the perfect man. As soon as he finds his feet upon the rock, Joshua offers up the kine, or his entire animal nature, before the ideal of the perfect man standing upon the rock of our salvation, or the Christ. Now all this happens in the immortal life field of Joshua. Does this not identify him with Jesus who gave his body to Christ in another incarnation?

But let us look farther before we judge. Several hundred years later we find in Zach. III: "And he showed me 'Joshua the High Priest, standing before the Angel of the Lord, and Satan standing at his right hand" (testing him), "and the Angel said unto Satan, 'The Lord rebuke thee Satan, yea the Lord that hath chosen Jerusalem" (peace), "rebuke thee, is not this a brand plucked out of the fire?"

"Now Joshua was clothed with filthy garments" (lower mind body), "and was standing before the Angel." Remember in his last incarnation he had offered up his desire nature, now it is the mind body that must be purified.

"And he answered and spake unto those that stood before him saying, 'Take those filthy garments from off him,' and unto him he said, 'Behold I have caused thine iniquity' (lower mind) 'to pass from thee, and I will clothe thee with rich apparel.'" (Wisdom.)

"And I said, 'Let them set a clean miter' (or diadem) 'upon his head.' So they set clean miter upon his head" (another symbol of crowning him with true wisdom), "and clothed him with garments" (gave him a purified mind body) "and the Angel of the Lord was standing by."

"And the Angel of the Lord protested" (spoke earnestly) "unto Joshua, saying 'Thus saith the "Lord of Hosts:" If thou wilt walk in my ways, and if thou will keep my charge, then thou shalt judge my house' (race), 'and shalt keep my courts' (take charge of the spiritual temples of the people, guard them), 'I will give thee a place of access among these that stand by.'" (He will let him come in between the two other Great Ones, the "Lord Jehovah" and the "Christ," the two who stand by.)

"Hear now, O Joshua the High Priest, thou and thy fellows that sit before thee (the other two Great Ones), for they are men that are for a sign" (or a wonder), "for behold I will bring forth My servant the Branch, for behold the Stone" (symbol of Mastership) "that I have set before Joshua" (the stone was set before Joshua in the last incarnation, remember); "upon one stone are seven eyes" (sight, or consciousness upon seven planes); "behold, I will engrave the graving thereof, saith the "Lord of Hosts"" (God in the heart), "and I will remove the iniquities of that land in one day" (he will be perfected in one incarnation, become a Master of Compassion, which really happened when he gave his body to the great Master Christ two thousand years ago.) How can it mean any other than our Blessed Jesus?

In Chapter IV we get another significant allegory:

"And the Angel that talked with me came again, and waked me as a man is wakened out of his sleep, and he said unto me, 'What seest thou?' And I said, I have seen and behold, a candlestick all of gold, with its bowl upon the top of it, and its seven lamps (seven races of men) thereon; there are seven pipes (streams of power) to each of the lamps, which are upon the top thereof; and two olive trees by it, one upon the right side of the bowl, and the other upon the left side thereof. And I answered and spake to the Angel that talked with me saying, 'What are these my Lord?' Then the Angel that talked with me answered and said unto me, 'Knowest thou not what these are?' And I said, 'No my Lord.' Then he answered and spake unto me, saying, 'This is the word of the Lord unto Zerubbable' (the great Initiator) 'saying, Not by might nor by power, but by My Spirit, saith the 'Lord of Hosts' (the God in the heart of every man). 'Who art thou, O great Mountain' (Mountain of the world's sin, or Karma) 'before Zerubbable? (he who was born at the gate of God or the gate of Initiation) 'thou' (the mountain of sin) 'shalt become a plain; and he shall bring forth the top stone' (Christ) 'with shoutings of Grace, Grace, unto it.'' Moreover the word of the Lord came unto me saying "The hands of Zerubbable" (he who was born at the gate of God) "have laid the foundation of this house" (the evolution of this great race), "his hands shall finish it; and thou shalt know that the Lord of Hosts hath sent me unto you. For who hath despised the day of small things?" (experiences of life) "for these seven" (races of men) "shall rejoice, and shall see the plumet in the hand of Zerubbable"; (The great Initiator shall measure and grade them according to their attainment, and ultimately all shall attain to the highest, so shall rejoice); "these are the eyes of God (the eyes in the stone, stone symbol of Master of Compassion, is here referred to, the seven eyes, sight on seven planes, the eyes of the God within the heart of man), "which run to and fro through the whole earth."

"Then I answered and said unto him, 'What are these two olive trees upon the right side of the candlestick and upon the left side thereof?' and I said a second time, 'what are these two olive branches, which are beside the two golden spouts, that empty the golden oil out of themselves?' and he answered me and said, 'Knowest thou not what these are?' and I said, 'No my Lord.' Then said he, 'These are the two anointed ones' (Jesus and the Christ) 'that stand by the Lord of the whole earth' (Lord Jehovah) Zach. IV. The three great manifestations of the Great Trinity whose mission it is to guide the race to their ultimate destiny, which is the same perfection that they themselves enjoy.)

Is it not plain to be seen that these three Great Ones are the manifestations of the Trinity? The "two anointed ones" being Jesus, whose work it is to teach man to purify and consecrate himself, thereby building up the soul, or the casual body in

CAN JESUS BE IDENTIFIED IN OTHER LIVES?

whose heart the Christ Child can be born by immaculate conception; Christ the "top stone," the "branch," "the root and the stem of David," both inspired by the bright and morning star, the IHVH, or the God within, that also flows through the Lord Jehovah who is here spoken of as the Lord of the whole earth, that is, the Lord of the Physical Plane. He guides the Monad in its descent into matter, and looks after its physical condition that it may have proper vehicles to manifest in, puts into the body a certain arrangement of atoms so that Spirit may make itself felt through the heavy matter; He gives to the race a moral code, then He turns them over to Jesus for further training along spiritual lines. Here is Jesus' place, mediator between man and God-Man, or Christ. Is it not a complete scheme. As above so below, we find this triplicity of arrangement everywhere, reaching down into the very atoms that form the basis of all manifestation. "How perfect are His works, His ways are past finding out!"

Let us take a look at Zach. vi, beginning at the ninth verse: "And the word of the Lord came unto me saying, 'Take of them of the captivity' (in the flesh), 'even of Heldai' (strength), 'of Tobijah' (good law), 'and Jedaiah' " (love); that is, take of the people those who are strong in the good law, and love and bring them to Initiation, for it goes on to say, "and come upon the same day, and go into the house of Josiah" (whom the Lord heals). "The son of Zephaniah" (hidden by the Lord), "whither they are come to Babylon" (the Gate of God or the gate of initiation), "yea take of them" (the initiates), "Silver" (redemption) "and Gold" (God's wisdom and righteousness), "and make crowns" (mark the plural, "crowns," not crown, because there are two heads to be crowned), "and set them upon the head of Joshua" (Jesus, the help of Jehovah) "the son of Jehozadak" (God justifies) "the High Priest; and speak unto him, saying, 'Thus speaketh the Lord of Hosts' " (the God inside, IHVH, and the God outside of man, the great Trinity, in One), saying, " 'Behold the man whose name is Branch' (Christ): and he shall grow up out of his place" (The One who is now the Christ was then occupying the place that Jesus now occupies) "he shall grow up out of his place, and he shall build the temple of the Lord," (He shall complete the Trinity of great workers, be the top stone capping the great temple, placed in the world for the salvation of man) "even he shall build the temple of the Lord; and he shall bear the glory, and shall sit and rule upon his throne; and He shall be a priest upon His throne; and the counsel of peace shall be between them both." (Between Jesus and Christ when they both use the same body and afterward work together to attain the same end, each in his appointed place, supplementing each other, each belonging to the same stem but the "Branch" shooting to the greatest height in the work. "And the crowns" (two of them) "shall be to Helem" (strength), "and to Tobijah" (good law), "and to Jedaiah" (love). "and to Hen" (rest, peace), "the son of Zephaniah" (hidden by the Lord, or a son of the Mystery worker), "for a memorial in the Temple of the Lord." That is, the two Great Ones shall be crowned by the redemption, and righteousness, of the Initiates that they have been instrumental in teaching the good law, strength, love, and peace, or harmony, in the Mysteries.

"And they that are far off" (younger races, and races to come) "shall come and shall build in the Temple of the Lord." (We are all being carved to be stones to be used in the Temple of God); "and ye shall know that the Lord of Hosts" (IHVH, the God within the heart, and the GOD without, the God in all things) "hath sent me to you."

In the next life of "Joshua" we all call him "Jesus," and we see the Christ grew up out of the place he held as Aaron, as prophesied, and we see him using a body prepared for him by Jesus ("the council of peace between them both"); he becomes the "Branch" with Jesus, and the crowns of redemption and righteousness are placed upon the heads of them both, and Jesus the mediator, the Great High Priest, and Christ our Lord, becomes to the people Jesus Christ; the two have been blended into one in the minds of the orthodox until they have lost the conception of the Blessed Trinity of Great Ones, each of whom is doing a certain work for the regeneration of man. The Lord Jehovah, the Master Jesus, and the Master Christ, each of them a Master, a perfect example of the ultimate attainment of the race, each ready always to utterly efface himself for the good of the race, all working in perfect harmony so that through them the great streams of IHVH, from the Supreme can flow, or the Solar Logos, perhaps I should say to be technically correct, for He ever "tempers the wind to the shorn lamb," and the mighty force of the great source is thus tempered by passing through the Great Ones until it is sufficiently attenuated so that our physical bodies may not be consumed when we receive the baptism. Remember Jesus is a type of the Masters, many of whom are now working with Him in the same line of work.

A most beautiful thought is, that when the western Christian prays, calling upon the Lord Jesus Christ, however ignorant he may be of these facts, he really calls upon the complete Trinity of Great Ones, whose duty it is to look after him in his triune development; thus does the good law hedge us about.

Does it not seem probable to the reader now, that, provided reincarnation is a fact, Isaac, Joshua, Joshua of Beth-Shemish, and Joshua the High Priest, were the same ego that reincarnated as Jesus of Nazareth? There is certainly a golden cord binding these characters of different ages together in a very striking way.

The Great Ones ever strive to hide their personality, being one with God, and one with us, even as they teach us to become one in them that we all may be one in God, as the Master Christ prayed that we should. The reader will remember the denial of John the Baptist that he was Elias, not that he meant to misstate, but that he wanted to impress upon them that it mattered not at all, who he was; his words show this motive, I am of no consequence in this matter, "I am a voice of one crying in the wilderness (of ignorance) "make His path straight." That was John's message, and he would give no other, nor would he gratify their curiosity. He wanted them to listen to the message. This alone stamps John as a great soul. So all of these Great Ones work in the secret place of the Most High.

CHAPTER XI.

ARE THESE SOME INCARNATIONS OF OUR BLESSED CHRIST?

It is with feelings of deepest humility and reverence that I submit my reasoning upon this mystic topic to the thinking public, knowing full well that it will seem the height of presumption to many consecrated souls, who are just as honest in their opposition, as I am in the stand that I take. To me these things are true. They have been an inspiration to me, so I fain would pass them on to assist others; but, before they leave my hands to start upon their long journey through many hands and many hearts, I feel like praying with Lord Francis Bacon: 'Thou, O Father, Who gavest the visible light as the first born of Thy creatures, and didst pour into man the intellectual light as the top and consummation of Thy Workmanship, be pleased to protect and govern this work, which cometh from Thy goodness and returneth to Thy glory.''

Above all things do I desire to exalt that Trinity of Beneficent Beings included in the words, the "Lord Jesus Christ," as uttered by the Christian. That it has been revealed to me that these are, in reality, three distinct personages, each perfect manifestations of the Trinity upon earth, is wondrous in my eyes, but I firmly believe it to be true. Three Great Ones, but one in the Father (the Logos); the Lord Jehovah; Jesus, that tender-hearted, compassionate Elder Brother, that ever-present help in time of trouble, that sweet sympathizer in all of our joys and fears; and that grand and glorious reality, the great Master Christ, who has made the whole world His fold, and who stays with suffering humanity to the end of the ages, inspiring the holiest aspirations of which we are capable. The truth, like a diamond, has many facets, and each view, no matter what may be the angle, shows forth a glory peculiarly its own, but in no way detracts from the other sides. Each is perfect in itself, yet the glory is far more resplendent when the jewel is lifted from the casket, that all of the facets may be seen at once. So with the Word of God, one age gets this view, another that, according to their evolution. In each age many different rays are discovered, all true, but all different, for not until the end of the ages will all of these be revealed, and the great Jewel lifted from the casket that the race with purified eyes may be able to see it in all of its glorious reality. Until then we may each add our mite to the light thrown in upon this wondrous gem, looking forward to the time when we shall be deemed worthy to be given a fuller view.

Because of the loss of the Mysteries to the Christian Church, occasioned by the worldly ambition that sprang up in that body, there is much confusion in the mind of the average Christian as to what is meant by the Second Person of the Trinity. If asked he will usually reply, "Why, Christ, of course," meaning the Man we know by that name.

We have tried to show in a preceding chapter, that the Great Trinity sends forth a triplicity of manifestations that manifest upon each plane, and at last gets down upon this dense Physical Plane, being transmitted through many different agents, for. thus does "He temper the wind to the shorn lamb"; "wind," His great force, and "shorn lamb," the lamb that was slain from the beginning of the world, or the spark of the Trinity embedded in the heart of every man, shorn of his heavenly estate until the end of the age of evolution. This is not a Biblical quotation, but the symbolism is the same.

"All things were made by Him, and without Him was not anything made that was made," we are told in John I, 1, and this refers to the great conception of the Second Person of the Trinity, the creative love wisdom aspect of God, in whom all of the universes live, and move, and have their being; but upon our own planet we have One that to us is more understandable, who gives to us this baptism, in whom we live, and move, and have our being, whom the Christians speak of as God, but whom the Theosophist calls the Solar Logos, a manifestation of this same creative Wisdom; and then comes that Great One who is closer still to us, who translates to us as much of this wondrous spiritual power as we are able to stand; this is the God Man, Christ, the great mediator between God and man. Many, many times has He incarnated in the flesh to help man to evolve, and we are what we are very largely because of His efforts. Because He is the perfect manifestation of this Trinity of forces that are latent in all mankind, and because He is one of our own humanity, He stands a perfect example of what we may all become, because of the Spirit inherent in us all, but He is not the Great Second Person of the Trinity. He is a manifestation of that force upon our lower plane, in the best form to assist mankind, a form that we may understand. He it was who entered the body of Jesus at the Baptism, and used the body three years.

The Lord Jehovah, Jesus, and the Christ represent to us the Holy Ghost, Son, and the Father, in their manifestations upon this planet. These three Great Ones come into direct contact with the race upon the lower planes, and contact man upon each of the three planes of his consciousness, the Physical, Moral, and Spiritual, according to the division of the work they are handling, as has been explained. This is repeated because it is so important that the reader keeps this distinction clearly before him.

With this conception well in mind, it is easy to see that none of the statements made about our Christ in Scripture are contradicted when examined by the new light shed upon the subject, but, upon the contrary, all becomes reasonable and luminous. Even as the Great Second Person of the Trinity, the "Word" of St. John, was the first begotten of the Father, so also was our Christ the first begotten of our race, to manifest the Father, the first born among many brethren. Even as the sun has always been the symbol of the great God, so has this symbol been always used to signify the Great Representative of that God among men, consequently the prophet says: "The Sun of righteousness will come with healing in his wings" (or rays). He is the "bright and morning star," the first star in the race to appear in its full brightness. He is the "way, the truth, and the life," in the sense that he has shown us by attaining, that the Divinity within us, as the Divinity within Him, is the way, the truth, and the life. "I am come in My Father's name, and ye receive Me not," he tells us in John v, 43. "Believest thou not that I am in the Father and the Father in me? The words that I say unto you I speak not from myself: but the Father abiding in Me doeth His works."

ARE THESE SOME INCARNATIONS OF OUR BLESSED CHRIST?

11. "Believe Me that I am in the Father, and the Father in Me: or else believe Me for the very works sake."

12. "Verily, verily, I say unto you, He that believeth in Me, the works that I do, shall he do also; and greater works than these shall he do; because I go unto the Father." John 14. (He becomes one with Him.)

St. Paul tells us, Gal. IV, 19, that he "travails in birth till the Christ be born in the hearts" of his followers, showing that he recognized this inner potential Divinity that they must awaken into life to attain. Also in Romans VIII, 14 to 18, he brings this out clearly.

So, dear Christian reader, do not be alarmed, lest any of the great conceptions that you may have entertained of the Great One will be disturbed by this investigation. Our Christ is far greater than you have dreamed of His being, unless you have been investigating along this line, because the Christians have lost the sublimer conception, and they have degraded the Great Second Person of the Trinity through lack of intelligent comprehension of the real immensity of the scheme. All additional light thrown upon the subject reveals Christ in His true exalted position, and all illumination makes it easier for Him to manifest His love to man, thus helping us to attain. He and Master Jesus (and the other Masters) represent to us the great Will, and Love and Wisdom aspect of God, even as the Lord Jehovah represents the activity aspect.

In saying that I find evidences of other incarnations of the Christ in the flesh in the Bible, I am agreeing with many of our most intelligent ministers of Christianity, and a few of them have been courageous enough to come boldly out with the statement. The Rev. Robert Stuart MacArthur, pastor of the Calvary Baptist Church, of New York City, said in a Christmas sermon preached in 1909, as reported in the newspapers: "The Son of God honored the world with frequent temporary incarnations before becoming the child of Mary in Bethlehem." * * * "The incarnate Word was the God-Man, having two names united in one personality." Jesus and Christ, the two names, or two individuals, united in one body. It is very apparent to the close student of philology that the Bible teaches the doctrine of reincarnation, and now the time seems to be ripe for Him to appear again, and some of us feel that we have received the command:

> "Tell ye the daughter of Zion (the consecrated soul)
> Behold thy King cometh unto thee,
> Meek and riding upon an ass,
> Upon a colt the foal of an ass."

Or in other words, He will come in a young physical body. Ass is an esoteric symbol of the physical. And the time will not be long.

In this allegorical reading the sons mentioned are those born of the Spirit. Physical relationship, being of minor importance, is not mentioned. "For they are not all Israel that are of Israel

7. Neither because they are Abraham's seed are they all children; but in Isaac shalt thy seed be called

8. That is, it is not the children of the flesh that are the children of God; but the children of the promise are reckoned for a seed." Romans ix, 6 and on.

To trace the incarnations of the Great One whom we call the "Christ" we will begin with Jacob, for that is the first of these lives that we identify in the Bible, and whether they were real incarnations or whether they are given us as types, the lesson is the same, and they teach reincarnation.

As shown in the lives of Jesus, the Great Initiate Paul states that the women spoken of in Gal. iv, 22, were covenants, and that Isaac is the child of the Spirit, not necessarily of the flesh; and so also is Jacob a spiritual son of Isaac and Rebecca. It will be recalled in this connection that Jacob tells Laban that he is the son of Rebecca, quite contrary to Oriental usage if he were the physical son, for such usage demanded the mention of the father first. Isaac is not even mentioned because Jacob is showing that Rebecca was his Alma Mater.

The Lord Jehovah commissions Abraham to lead the great Aryan race (not simply the Jews), and gives him the Second Great Initiation, the one that shows that the desire nature must have been conquered, and after that episode the child Isaac is born of the Spirit. That is, Isaac is a young student aspiring to Initiation, who develops under the tutelage of Abraham. He may have been a physical son, but that is not at all necessary.

ARE THESE SOME INCARNATIONS OF OUR BLESSED CHRIST?

Abraham sees that the conditions are not just what they should be for the young spiritual aspirant, so he sends a faithful servant to the "White Brother" (Laban), a member of the Great White Lodge evidently, the son of Bethuel (dweller in God), for some teachers for the promising young Isaac, and the servant leaves the matter entirely in the hands of God. He is guided to some wells (of wisdom), where he finds Rebecca drawing the water (of wisdom) for her father's flock, and is so pleased with the way she does it, that he inquires and finds that the school is under the care of the very Bethuel, and Laban, whom he is seeking. Whether the servant studies until he masters the wisdom of the school, and then returns, or whether he takes teachers back with him qualified to establish Mystery work such as Laban had, in his classes ranked as "sister," is not plain; but probably it was done in the latter way, as he is represented as returning without delay. An any rate, when Isaac was forty, or had the perfected physical development, as indicated by the quaternary, the higher wisdom "Rebecca," came hidden behind her veil (a common symbol of the inner Mystery work), and as soon as he saw her, he loved her. Keep in mind that we found in this character indications that he was an incarnation of Jesus, not Christ. The old school, Sarah, was dead, or he had outgrown its teachings, and was lonely, or reaching out for something more. These allegories all have the double meaning of referring not only to the life of the individual, but also to that of the race that he leads, so here the man, Isaac, gets his Mystery teaching, but at the same time the Mystery teaching of the Great White Lodge is established upon a new and firmer footing among the young race that is growing into a strong and formidable people, and Isaac the Initiate is its leader.

From this race, under the teaching of the school of wisdom thus established, comes forth first a great exoteric worker, a leader in ritualistic service among the masses; and almost at the same time, close upon his heels comes forth another, of a very different type, altogether different from the first; one who is to start the new great fifth root race (Aryan race) upon its spiritual path in a very definite manner. Esau is a distinct advance upon the old type, the fourth root race, and starts the fourth and a half root race, a race that dominated the Orient for ages, and showed great promise from a physical standpoint, so much so, that the father (the old race) was blind to the degenerate tendencies that are shown in the allegorical marriages, that "were a bitterness of spirit to Isaac and Rebecca," for he showed such an inclination to degrade himself by making ties beneath his station, or in other words, he showed a tendency to revert to old traditions rather than adopt the new and progressive ones that were upheld by the Rebecca school. He is a "great hunter before the Lord" we are told, so he was very strong and aggressive in his religious work, and the people take him to be the greater of the two brothers. They like his venison, or the fruit of his activities, and he works hard and willingly to get their praise and blessing. He is shown, however, to be a slave to the desire body, when hungry will give even his birthright for a mess of pottage, rather than suffer the pangs of hunger. He thinks he will die if he denies his body, while Jacob shows the strong characteristic of the new fifth root race in being able to control his desire, for the sake of future advantage. Self control and the ability to look forward with intelligent comprehension of cause and effect, are the peculiar traits of the fifth root race.

Jacob differs from Esau in many ways. He is not hairy (not strongly physical), he loves the tabernacle (loves religious study and meditation), is a favorite with his mother (the Mystery school), and he is obedient to the dictates of his teachers, even when told to assume the physical characteristics of Esau, humbling himself to cater to the common people and persuades them to eat of the goat (a sin offering) instead of the venison of Esau's hunt, or the material reward that he presented them, and Jacob gets the blessing, because in their blindness they do not discover his real intentions.

Isaac was the perfected quaternary (symbol of the perfected physical) when Rebecca came, but when the boys are born he is three-score, or he has entered the spiritual triangle. Spirituality is well developed in the inner work of the race. Rebecca had been but a sister of Laban, not one of his advanced classes, and for a long time no very earnest students came from her; even now Esau is much more material than spiritual, he realizes the force of religion for power, but has no thought of using it to purify himself. His desire nature is dominant.

Jacob, true to the name, becomes the supplanter of Esau in

every way, and becomes the head of the great fifth root race (Aryan). His mother, who sees that the struggle with Esau (unbalanced forces) may kill out his spirituality, insists that he be sent to Bethuel (dweller in God) and Laban (White Brother) for further illumination along higher lines.

All of the words used in these tales are so suggestive of deep meaning that it takes great self control to pass them by. We can, however, handle but a few because of lack of space.

Jacob was going from Beer-Sheba (well of an oath, well means wisdom) towards Haran (spiritual heights).

Remember that "Rock," "stone," is a symbol of the Master of Compassion. "They did drink of the spiritual rock that followed them and the rock was Christ." I Cor. 10.

Jacob lies down with his head upon a stone, or with his head resting, or reflecting, upon the possibilities of his becoming a Master, for that, he knows, is the purpose of his special instruction, and he has a vision. He sees what seems to be a long ladder reaching up to heaven, and angels ascending and descending upon it. He was evidently given a view of the evolution of man, the descent of the ego into incarnation, and its evolution back to God. "The land as thou liest," or the plane you see as you lie, or the plane of consciousness that you have, that enables you to see this, "To thee and to thy see will I give it." It is the birthright of the fifth root race, and they will eventually gain it; "and thy seed shall be as the dust of the earth, and thou shalt spread abroad to the west, to the east, to the north, to the south, and in thee, and in thy seed, shall *all* the families of the earth be blessed." Not only will he be the great leader of the religions of the world during the fifth root race but he is training the leader of the sixth root race as well, as will develop later, so all nations and races will be blessed. "And behold I am with thee and will keep thee whithersoever thou goest, and will bring thee again"; that is, you are now given a glimpse of this plane of consciousness, but you will develop until you will be able to function consciously upon this plane all of the time. "I will bring thee again to this place."

He is told that it is the "Lord Jehovah" who is talking with him, that he was the God of Abraham, and of Isaac, and that now he will be the God of Jacob. Possibly Christ was thinking of this vision when later He said to the Jews in Palestine, "What saith your Scriptures?" God is the God of Abraham, Isaac, and Jacob; God is the God of the living not of the dead." "And (Jacob) was afraid, and he said, surely IHVH (Jehovah) is in this place, and I knew it not"; that is, he had not before realized that IHVH was really within his own heart. Undoubtedly, also, he saw, to some extent, what the future had in store for him. So he sets the "stone" he had under his head (or the idea of masterhood that he had been thinking of) up as a pillar in Bethel (the Temple of God, which is his heart), as a permanent memorial of his intention to attain that ideal. He anoints it with the oil of consecration, and from that moment is the disciple bound by his oath to attain Mastership. He has heard the call and has answered, "Lo, I come to do Thy will, O God!"

Now, he takes up his journey towards the east, or towards intellectual understanding, until he comes to the well (of wisdom) of Laban, the White Brother. Here Laban is called the son of Nahor, while Isaac called him the son of Bethuel, the dweller in God. As Nahor means "snorter," and as this is a term sometimes used in India to indicate a Yoga, or one who practices the breathing exercises, possibly this is the significance of the term as used here.

Jacob finds the wells (of wisdom) all covered with stones (Masters of wisdom), and he sees Rachel, clear-eyed, beautiful Rachel, watering her father's flock; or he sees and desires the attainment of the higher wisdom, that he sees given to certain of the people by the school called Rachel, or the particular system that she typifies. Rachel is evidently not a Hebrew name, but may come from "Ra" and "Chela"; it is at any rate very ancient. Being feminine in gender, we may translate it God's productive pupil; the Hebrew translates it, the ewe, or the productive sheep; as sheep is a smybol of the Israelite, or the spiritual part of the race, it is not so far off. The productive part of the spiritual part of race, would be a very fair description of the work that Rachel stood for.

Rachel is a younger daughter. The more advanced work is always the last to develop. Jacob serves seven years which seem but a day, because of the love he bears the clear-eyed, beautiful, wisdom, serving faithfully, studying hard, and gaining possessions

ARE THESE SOME INCARNATIONS OF OUR BLESSED CHRIST?

(intellectual and spiritual possessions), by hook or by crook, in every possible way; but at the end of the seven years finds he has married, or mastered, only Leah (the weak eyed); that is, he can not yet see upon the higher planes, as these schools always taught those pupils who were qualified to do. So Laban explains that the lower work (Leah) is always taken first, before one can be given the higher instruction, but that now he can enter the school of Rachel. He will, however, be obliged to serve, or study here, also, seven years, before he will have all that the school can give him.

So another seven years of study and of teaching follows, for all of the time he tends flocks, or looks after the welfare of the people, and during the last seven years he selects the strongest and best of Laban's people and makes them his by the treatment he gives them, and no matter how often the flock is changed upon him, invariably the strongest and best, the most evolved, are found to be followers of Jacob, and he gains great possessions, both in flocks and herds (pupils and followers), and in gold (wisdom), jewels (righteousness), and riches (understanding). That is, he has gained greatly in wisdom, righteousness, and understanding, and has a large following of pupils. All of the most evolved and strongest of the people flock to Jacob, recognizing in him their natural leader.

He places in their watering-troughs rods made of the plane tree, or holds before them in his wisdom teaching the use of the rod of Initiation in opening up the consciousness to the different planes of consciousness, and encourages them to look forward to the Initiations as a definite goal; and they become ring streaked, and spotted, or more highly developed in spots and streaks.

Laban sees his authority slipping away, and tries to discover the secret that he perceives Jacob has gained, but when Jacob takes him into the tabernacle of Rebecca she sedately sits with his Gods hidden beneath her skirts after the manner of women, or Mystery work, and he finds himself no wiser than before She cannot divulge to this representative of the old race those things that only the more evolved of the new race can understand. He would not be able to grasp them.

Laban is obliged to admit himself beaten, but as God had warned him in a dream not to interfere with the development of the new race, he partakes of the sacrament with its leader, they mutually agree to be friendly, and Laban goes back to his own country, or settles back to his own state of consciousness, realizing that a new race is being born, and that he must be content to see his people depart from him, as they come into the broader realization. Jacob had tried for six years to work with him, but continual misunderstandings had been the result, and Jacob says, "I will arise and go to my Father," so after the covenant with Laban he is free to continue his journey.

But Jacob finds that he must not only part peaceably with the old school, but he must also forgive his brother before he can see his father's face. All night long he struggles with the angel, his higher self, and only as the higher self kills out all selfish desire, symbolized by the withered thigh, only then does he "conquer with God," and become fit to enter the great Buddhic Plane, the plane watered by the great Euphrates (the great and abounding river of wisdom and love). Upon this plane only universal love can stand, and when that enters the heart, then Jacob conquers with God. Still the fear of his brother is not entirely taken from him, but he finds that when he goes to him in the new spirit, that has sprung up in his heart, his brother is at once made his friend, and he has nothing to fear.

Thus is the Mystery work of the great fifth root race started by the Great One who is to be the spiritual leader of it during all the ages, while as yet but few had evolved far enough to be really classed fifth race people. This all happened while the fourth race was prospering, and while the great Buddha was acting as spiritual leader of that race, just as now Master Moro and Master Koot Hoomi are selecting those who are sufficiently evolved to start the sixth root race type. Ages must elapse before the type will be the ruling one in humanity, but the Masters work with infinite patience and love, age after age, and the first day of the work is as sacred in their eyes as is the work of the last or the full grown race.

We find that Leah bears many children. The lower or exoteric understanding of the new race's religious views takes with many; but Rachel is barren for many years. The Inner Mystery work needs a high state of development, not easily obtained at that stage of the world; but at last two spiritual sons are born, Joseph, whose name indicates an increase in consciousness, and Benjamin, who is evidently a new impulse given to the old religion of the day, for Gautama Buddha, later on, comes as a son of Benjamin, in the Bible.

All of the sons of Israel are spiritual sons or efforts to establish religions in the different nations, in different incarnations of the Great One Himself, and they extend over considerable time. In the poem called the "Blessing of the Sons of Israel," there are indications of this, as we will see later.

Joseph is shown to be psychic from the start, and has a vision in which he sees the sun (Christ), and the moon (Lord Jehovah), and the other stars of which he is one (the other Masters) bow down to him. Surely this can be no other than Master Koot Hoomi.

Israel makes for Joseph a coat of many colors (teaches him to purify his vehicles), and the brethren throw him into a pit filled with the slime of their own jealousy. From here they sell him into the bondage of Egypt, or the physical, making the father believe that the spiritual nature has been killed by the lower self, that the coat of many colors has been defiled with the blood of animals. But after many trials that show the integrity of the character of Joseph, he conquers the flesh, and stands a victor, able to hand out spiritual bread to his brothers in their time of stress.

In his old age we find Israel dwelling in Goshen (God's peace), in the midst of Egypt (the Physical Plane people), while Joseph gives to the brethren the spiritual food, and loving care of an older brother. Joseph gives out bread to all of the people of the land, only stipulating that the people bring their flocks and herds or the common people that he may have the care of them in order to instruct them; for there was a great famine (of intellectual and spiritual things) in the land of Canaan (the low-lying land, the land of the lower planes of consciousness).

In Oriental countries it has always been customary for the eldest born of the male children to be given the father's blessing, but here the spiritual nature of the tale is shown by the fact that Israel deliberately blesses the one who represents the greatest spiritual development, preferring him to the one who symbolizes mentality (Mannassah, probably from the Aryan word Manus, mind). He gives his strongest blessing to Ephraim (double fruitfulness, or fruitfulness of both mental and spiritual natures).

We must hasten, but will tarry a moment to examine that ancient poem where Israel is shown as blessing his sons. The sons are really spiritual impulses given to the religions of the world, or new religions started by his spiritual sons, or Initiates, or by himself in his different incarnations.

"Reuben thou art my first born, my might and the beginning of my strength; the pre-eminence of dignity, and the pre-eminence of power. Unstable as water (controlled by desire) "thou shalt not succeed." The sea is a symbol of the Desire Plane.

Simeon and Levi are condemned because they are too violent and self willed, they but hock the ox (their animal nature), when they should kill it out, or offer it entirely to the Lord. Judah is born under Leo, "the Lion's Whelp," and shall be famous, because from him shall come the Great Ones who shall rule the races until Shiloh come, or until the rest time comes. As a matter of fact, Christ, Jesus, and Master Koot Hoomi the Christ of the sixth root race, all came through this line in the David incarnation. He binds his ass's foal to a vine; that is, he binds his animal nature down by tying it strongly to the spiritual, and washes his garments in the blood of the grape, or washes his subtile bodies in spirituality.

"Dan" (Samson came from Dan) "shall judge his people as one of the tribes of Israel."

"Dan shall be a serpent" (wisdom) "in the way,
That biteth the horses heels
So that the rider falleth backward."

That is, Samson, the serpent of wisdom, shall cripple the animal nature so that the rider, or the man, shall draw back from his material desires in the journey of life.

In Asher, I think I perceive a later incarnation of the Christ than the Bible mentions elsewhere, so perhaps it is just as well to leave it out of this study.

"Joseph" (increased, Master Koot Hoomi) "is a fruitful bough, the son of a fruitful tree" (great teacher) "by a fountain" (of wisdom).

"His daughters" (his Mystery work) "run over the wall"

(of the consciousness of the fifth root race, because he will train the sixth root race). "His hands are made strong by the Mighty One of Jacob" (the same IHVH that has been the strength of Jacob). "From thence is the Shepherd the "Stone of Israel" (the Jesus incarnation is in direct line from Joseph through Solomon, Master Koot Hoomi).

"The blessings of thy father" (Israel or Christ)
"Have prevailed above the blessings of my progenitors
Unto the utmost bounds of the everlasting hills";

(he will be guiding the race until the very end of the ages, for as the Messiah of the sixth root race he will be still guiding his people while the seventh root race is forming and living its life, just as Christ is guiding the fifth root race while the fourth root race is with us to be also guided, and the sixth is being started. Surely unto the utmost bounds of the everlasting hills will be his dominion. What a tremendous responsibility!)

Benjamin, afterward Hindooism, "is a wolf that raveneth" or that swallows everything in sight, and that is the characteristic of that religion in after years, taking and appropriating every idea that came and making it its own. Today it does the same. "In the morning" (while it is young) "he shall devour the prey, but in the evening he shall divide the spoil with other religions.

No one knows who penned this poem, but that it is simply a blind, giving identification, esoterically, to the incarnations of the Christ of the fifth root race, the great religious leaders that He trained, and the great religious movements that were either started by Him or in which He took a prominent part, is without doubt true. There were twelve of these spiritual impulses—the sacred number of completion

In time the Children of Israel, or the spiritual minded of the new race, grew and multiplied, until the Egyptians (the Physical Plane people) became fearful that they might conquer them, so the great battle between Spirit and matter began in the race, even as it had been fought in the hearts of the redeemed of the race. Thus do the cycles of the great races of humanity follow in the order that they register in the life of man. The Moses stories show this mighty struggle, and trace the dealings of the Great Helpers as they guided out of the bondage of Egypt (or the dense physical), through the wilderness (of ignorance and delusion), through the Jordan (of the degenerative tendencies of the strongly developed desire nature), and into the Promised Land (of extended consciousness, and inner peace), the few who were ready to follow the law that enabled them to thus attain.

As our Blessed Lord said in His Krishna birth, "Whenever there is decay of righteousness, and there is exaltation of unrighteousness, then I Myself come forth."

"For the protection of the good, for the destruction of evil doers, for the sake of firmly establishing righteousness, I am born from age to age." (The Bhagavad Gitâ, Fourth Discourse, 7 and 8.)

Consequently when the time came in the development of race when the great struggle was to take place, when the powers of evil were mustering their forces for a strong stand to prevent the regenerating process from accomplishing its destiny, then do we find our Great Helper coming down into the bondage of the flesh again for our sakes, again crucified upon the cross of dense matter to assist man to rise above the bondage of the physical, to liberate the souls in the prison house of flesh.

In the Aaron incarnation Christ comes from the tribe of Levi, "The Lion of the tribe of Judah, I will divide them in Jacob" (the physical part of the race), "and scatter them in Israel" (the spiritual part of the race). Aaron is called to assist his brother Moses, when four-score and three years old, the four denoting the completed quaternary, and the three the perfected triangle or the Trinity.

Moses is four-score, or the perfected physical, the quaternary, although the Lord has told him that he is to act as "God to the people," and he shows his double commission by administering the rites of Initiation to Joshua, to Aaron, and to Eleazar. To Joshua (Jesus) he gave the Second Great Initiation in that incarnation, and to Aaron and Eleazar (Master Koot Hoomi) the third. In this incarnation Christ is acting in the place that has since been held by Jesus; that is, in the second degree of the work of the great Trinity, that symbolized by the letter H, in the four letters IHVH. VH, we must remember, handles man upon the Physical Plane, and is managed by the Lord Jehovah, but the first H signifies the creative love wisdom of the higher

ARE THESE SOME INCARNATIONS OF OUR BLESSED CHRIST?

planes, and that department of the work is to evolve the soul or causal body. At the time Aaron worked with Moses, He (Christ) occupied this place, and the great Lord Buddha, called Melchizedek in the Bible, occupied the place since occupied by the Christ.

The Bible student will at once recall the words of St. Paul, that Great Initiate, whom all of the different schools of thought recognize as an authority upon occult matters, in Heb. VII: "For this Melchizedek, king of Salem (peace), priest of God Most High (El Shadai), who met Abraham returning from the slaughter of the kings, and blessed him, to whom also Abraham divided a tenth part of all, being first, by interpretation, King of Righteousness, then also King of Salem, which is King of Peace; without father, without mother, without genealogy, having neither beginning of days nor end of life, but made like unto the Son of God, abideth a priest continually."

"4. Now consider how great this man was, unto whom Abraham the patriarch, gave a tenth." Then he goes on to show how Levi was yet unborn, for he was to descend through the line of Abraham.

7. "But without any dispute the less is blessed of the greater."

8. "And here men that die receive tithes, but there One, of whom it is witnessed that he liveth."

15. "And what we say is yet more abundantly evident, if after the likeness of Melchizedek there ariseth another priest" (Christ) "who hath been made, not after the law of carnal commandment, but after the power of an endless life; for it is witnessed of Him, Thou are a priest forever after the order of Melchizedek."

In Hebrews IX, 28, Paul shows that he comprehended the double duty that our Christ did in the Trinity of Great Helpers, by serving in the place that Jesus has since occupied, before becoming the Messiah: "So Christ also, having been once offered to bear the sins of many" (or bear with the sins of many), "shall appear a second time apart from sin, to wait for him unto salvation." That is, He shall appear in the highest position of Spirit, the part of the Trinity of workers symbolized by the letter "I," Yod, when He will manifest the perfected Trinity. In Him is the Temple of God on earth completed, the IHVH, Jehovah, the Great, manifested in perfection in the three Great Ones,

Christ "I," Jesus "H," Lord Jehovah "VH," three in one Spirit, each perfect, but each having a different and distinct line of work to do in the great plan of evolution.

Let us not forget when our brother, the Hindoo, worships the Buddha, that the Great One is the Melchizedek, that our Abraham thought it worth while to pay tithes to, and that St. Paul recognizes as the predecessor of our Blessed Lord.

In Numbers III, 2, 3, it will be noticed that the sons are clearly the spiritual sons of Aaron, not the sons of the flesh. "These are the names of the sons of Aaron; Nadab, the first born, and Abihu, Eleazar, and Ithama. These are the sons of Aaron, the priests that were anointed, whom he consecrated to minister in the priest's office." The first two, we are told, died because "they offered unworthy sacrifice unto the Lord." Plainly the passage is to be read from the spiritual standpoint. The Hebrew Kabbalah, as translated by S. L. M. Mathers, says, page 176, paragraph 529: "Whosoever descendeth from his former position wherein he was before, concerning such an one is it said in Scripture that he died."

In Leviticus XXIV, 2, we have the commission of Aaron to serve as the great supply of spiritual strength to the race from the evening (of lack of understanding) until the morning (of regeneration of the race). "Command the Children of Israel" (those of the Aryan race who are guided by the Divinity within) "that they bring unto thee pure olive oil, beaten for light" (assist him with spiritual impulses) "to cause the lamp to burn continuously, without the Veil of the Testimony" (keep a strong spiritual impulse in the ritualistic service of the people in their Church work), "in the tent of the meeting shall Aaron keep it in order from evening" (of lack of discernment of the race) "to morning" (of enlightment), "before Jehovah *continually*, and it shall be a statute *forever* throughout your generations" (throughout the incarnations of your race). "He shall keep in order the lamps upon the pure candlestick before Jehovah continually." Note the words "forever" and he is to do this "continually." This is not a matter that is to change with the changing customs, it is not something to be disturbed by the downfall of nations, or the destruction of temples; he is to continue it forever, and keep at it continually. As they have no word that gives exactly the same meaning that we have attached to forever, perhaps it would be nearer the truth to translate it to the end of the ages.

Here we have the same idea that Zechariah IV, 2, brings out in his vision of the great candlestick having seven lamps (seven races of men), fed from founts of two Great Ones that he saw as olive trees "upon the left hand and upon the right." "And I answered and said unto him, what are these two olive branches upon the left side and upon the right that supply the lamps of the golden oil" (wisdom) "out of themselves? and he answered and said unto me, knowest thou not what these are? and I said, No, My Lord, and he answered and said unto me these are the two Great Ones" (Christ and Jesus) "that stand by the Lord of the whole earth" (the Lord Jehovah).

Numbers III, 5: "And Jehovah spake unto Moses saying: Bring me the tribe of Levi and set before Aaron the priest, that they may minister unto him, and they shall keep his charge, and the charge of the whole congregation to do the service of the Tabernacle." (They were to take charge of the religious work upon earth to be the servers under the Great Ones of the H, or creative wisdom department, who would in turn supply them with spiritual inspiration, that would lead them to build up their souls, or causal bodies (tabernacles) and assist others to do the same, for that is the work of this department.)

9. "And thou shalt appoint Aaron and his sons and they shall keep their priesthood."

Numbers IV, 16, we find the right of succession again recognized for Master Koot Hoomi in the words. "And the charge of Eleazar son of Aaron shall be for oil and light" (he shall help supply the spiritual power), "and the sweet incense" (love and prayer), "and the continual meal offering" (attend to the sacrifices in the spirit), "and the anointing oil" (wisdom), "and the charge of the Tabernacle" (he will have the succession to the place in the Great Temple of the Lord, of the anointed one, to be one of the Great Three who manifest the Trinity to man). At one time this Trinity was Melchizedek, our Christ, and Lord Jehovah. Now it is Christ, Jesus (and the other Masters), and Lord Jehovah; if Occultists are right and we are reading these allegories right, in the sixth race this Mighty Three will be Master Koot Hoomi. If Jesus has a successor I have not identified him, and so will keep him in his present place, as He is very evidently a type of the Masters, who as a whole occupy this place; but it seems plain that Master Moro (Abraham) will occupy the place of the Lord Jehovah for the sixth root race. It will be remembered that when Moses initiated Aaron in the Mount, that Aaron took off his priestly robes and placed them upon the shoulders of Eleazar (Master K. H.), who had also taken the Third Great Initiation with him.

If the Great White Lodge is an existing institution, as all of the sacred Scriptures seem to indicate, if the Initiations have been given to man all the way along as soon as he was ready, then reincarnation is a positive necessity to give man the opportunity to attain the proper qualifications to make such a thing possible; and if this is the way it works out, then, surely, all of these indications point to Aaron being an incarnation of the Christ. Otherwise, how account for these things? If one divests the mind of the bondage of the old chronological table, and remembers that this is the history of the unfoldment of the spiritual natures of the great leaders of the whole race, not of the Jews only, it will be much easier to grasp that these are allegories that bring out those typical stages in the life of an Initiate, that will ultimately be experienced by each of us as we advance.

The next incarnation of the Great One, who always returns when man needs him most, is to be found in the character of Samson. This allegory must be very old. Many of the words are so ancient that all trace of their original meanings have been lost. The local coloring of Palestine was given it by some compiler, probably Ezra, to cultivate that spirit of patriotism that was so needed, if the Jews were again to become an independent nation, but I surmise that the events took place upon the plains, and in the mountains of India in a very distant time.

Remember that most of these personal nouns have a double meaning, one applying to an individual and one to the race, tribe, or organization that that individual stands for. So Israel, while a man, is also the great Aryan race, not the Jews. Judah stands for the Jews. When used in some connections Israel refers to the spiritual part of the race, and Jacob to the Physical Plane part of them. The Philistines were the descendants of the fourth and a half root race, which is symbolized by Esau. The word means travelers, and is sometimes used simply to note those who are progressing, regardless of nation or tribe.

For ages the race spoken of as the Philistines really dominated the Orient. They were the merchants and traders, the great materialistic thinkers, the great warriors, the active, alive, dominant people. The young fifth root race were also strongly physical in their development, all of its physical forces were virile and active, only here and there one became conscious of the Spirit within struggling for utterance, and such, as a rule, sought religious communities, or took the Nazerite vow, devoting their lives to the instruction of others. These little Schools of the Prophets were to be found scattered all over the hills in sequestered places, and are, even to this day, although in a far less degree.

The god "Dagon," worshiped by the Philistines, half fish half man, is a perfect symbol of a god of desire, for the symbol of the Desire Plane is the sea. We find the materialistic Philistines worshipping the god of desire, and Israel, the nation, having sinned, are under their dominion for forty years (again the completed quaternary). Just at this time once more is the Great Helper found in a fleshly body. Again does he come to extricate man from his spiritual difficulties.

The reader will remember that we discovered that the sun is used to symbolize the one occupying the position that our Christ occupies today, but at that time Melchizedek held that chair, although the succession was understood by Initiates. Samson (little sun)—the name establishes the identity of the ego—is son of a mother who is visited by an angel and is sufficiently evolved so that she can carry on a conversation with the supernatural visitor, something that takes practice, as Occultists know. She is the wife of "Manoah," whose name means peace, and she is told to purify herself, and touch no meat, or wine, or unclean thing, to go near no dead body, and to devote herself to the Lord, for she who has been barren is to bear a child, who is to be a Nazerite from his birth. Note the restrictions imposed upon her, for they also will be in full force upon the Nazerite from birth, and in addition to those named he must be a celibate.

Manoah belongs to the tribe of Dan, of whom Israel prophesied Dan shall be a serpent (wisdom) in the path (of the race), and

AN ESOTERIC READING OF BIBLICAL SYMBOLISM

the serpent shall bite the heels of the horses (the animal nature), so that the rider falleth backward. That is, wisdom (H) shall check the progress of the animal nature in its desires.

Let us look for a moment at this beautiful little love story by which child man might get in the literal reading a sweet and pure idea of love and fidelity. Manoah, the peaceful man with his loving wife, who is so pure that the angels of heaven come to converse with her. When she gets the vision she at once confides in her husband and he accepts the story with unwavering trust, thinking only the the responsibility of the charge. Note how he at once begins to pray that the angel may come and tell them how to care for the little one who is of sufficient importance for such unusual steps to be taken to secure proper conditions. Again the angel comes in response to this request, and again it is to the wife that he appears; but in response to her request, he kindly stays while she goes to call her husband, and then, when the man would have offered hospitality in true Oriental fashion, showing that his mind dwelt upon material things more than his wife's, the angel showed his nature by ascending in the flame, thus showing himself a Sun Spirit. The story is a beautiful one and reminds one of the birth of Jesus, and of John the Baptist. The spiritual significance as well as the literal facts being very plain.

Now let us note some of the points that give us the key to the inner meaning of the allegories connected with the mysterious character that we call Samson, that the orthodox will tell you drank, and associated with bad women, but that the account tells us "pleased God mightily." Surely there is a misunderstanding somewhere. We note that the home of Manoah, the home of peace, was between "Zorah," the place of hornets, or the hornets' nest (materialists are good home-makers but their tongues sometimes have a sting), and "Eshtaol, which means petition, prayer; so this home of peace lay between intense physical activity, and prayer. Here it was that "the Lord began to move the child."

Before going farther let us stop and consider what it meant to be a Nazerite from birth. From the earliest records preserved to the race from any source, we infer that the Nazerite was an old and established custom of recognition of the power and the sanctity of certain individuals, who incarnated from time to time, who took the vow of Nazerite, in order to be released from the ordinary routine of physical existence, to attend entirely to the affairs of God. The word is derived from Nazar, or serpent, a name given to the ancient wise men.

There were two kinds of Nazerites, distinguished as the Nazerite of days and the Nazerite from birth. The Nazerite of days was one who took an oath for a certain time, until some deed be accomplished, after which he could go to the priest and have his head shaved and after offering sacrifices be absolved from further abstinence, and austerities, and go home and follow his ordinary occupation, except that he was supposed always, thereafter, to lead an exemplary life. But the Nazerite from birth was supposed to be consecrated by his parents, because of some understanding that such was the desire of the ego that was about to incarnate. Often was the end attained by a vision, or by some supernatural occurrence. The vow of the Nazerite from birth was as solemn as that given the Great High Priest, and any violation of the vow took as serious a ceremonial as they used to reinstate a Great High Priest. It looks as though the great Venus souls who came so many times to assist infant humanity, may have instituted the custom to protect themselves from the common material life of the people, while they stayed in the flesh to teach man. The people understood that the Nazerite was to be fed and clothed by any one of whom it was asked, for he was the messenger of God and must not be troubled with material considerations. He dressed in a certain way, and always wore his hair long. By this were they known. He was vowed to celibacy; he must keep himself pure from all defilement; must not go near a dead body, not even that of his own father, or mother, and, if by accident he should touch a dead body, a very strict ceremonial must be gone through with, before he could again serve the Lord. He was vowed to the continual service of God, and as the servant of the Most High, he must keep himself absolutely pure. For the purpose of securing this desirable result every detail of his life was scrupulously dictated. He must bathe daily, he must touch no wine, not even the fruit of the grape, he must eat no flesh, nor ever touch a dead body or a carcass.

Let us keep these things in mind as we study, and see if we can not find a meaning that will reconcile in our minds Samson's being "mighty with the Lord."

In the first allegory in Judges xiv, 2, 7, we find him asking his parents to get a wife for him, of the daughters of Timnath, or a portion of the Philistines. He, the Nazerite, asking for a wife! Now we notice that his parents do not remind him of his vow, but object on the ground that the daughters of his own people should satisfy him; evidently it is not a question of physical women at all, but one concerning schools of Mystery, which were called women, widows, wives, concubines, sisters, daughters, according to the estimation in which they were held by the hierophant in charge of them, or the peculiar system of their teachings Not only is Samson not reproved by his parents for breaking his vow in wanting a wife, but the Lord is shown as approving, in the words, Judge 14, 4: "For his father and mother knew not it was of the Lord"; so the Lord was leading him. Certainly the Lord would not lead Samson to break the very solemn oath he had taken to remain pure in His service.

He insists that they go down to Timnath for him; that is, take steps to get the school for him; and he goes to the vineyards, or to spiritual exercises, to prepare himself for the new duty. Remember he is under oath to touch no grapes, and the vineyard was a common symbol referring to the cultivation of spirituality.

Here he meets a young lion roaring against him (his own animal nature), and he slays it with no weapon. Then he, the Nazerite, is pictured as taking honey out of the carcass of that dead lion and eating it, absolutely an impossibility for a Nazerite, if taken literally; yet we are assured that the Lord was "with him mightily." Can the reader not perceive the symbol? From the slain animal nature, is taken the sweet fruits of the spirit, that he not only enjoys himself, but gives to his parents, and they too enjoy the spiritual food. From the dead animal nature is the spirit fed.

"In the Leontica or Lion grade of Mithriaca there was a honey rite." (Mysteries of Mithra, by G. R. S. Mead, page 60.)

Samson has had a great spiritual baptism, and his soul overflows with the desire to give to others, so he goes to the school, evidently rather to impart to them of his riches, than to receive of them, for his conundrums show his desire to test them as to their knowledge in symbols and Mystery work. They cannot tell what he means by "out of the eater came forth meat, out of the strong came forth sweet." They attempt to take advantage of him in unfair ways rather than own that they do not comprehend, and when he perceives this spirit of being loath to acknowledge that any one knows more than themselves, he turns the tables upon them and tells them such truths that he slays (conquers) thirty of them, and takes their garments, or their arguments, and sends them back at the others, to satisfy them; but this spirit of unteachable hostility tries him and he leaves them, and the wife instead of going to the home of her husband as she would have done had it been a physical marriage stays with her father and is given to his friend.

His wife beseeching him seven days to reveal his secret, and at last succeeding only to betray him, shows he had some method of Mystery work that he tried upon them, but found them untrustworthy. After a time he goes back with a kid, symbolic of a sin offering, but he is not allowed to enter the Mystery work, so he then thinks up another plan of reaching the people.

Now comes the fox story that has so puzzled the people of the ages since the Mysteries have been lost to Christianity. Let us stop a moment and consider what use a fox would naturally play in an allegory. A fox is considered the most cunning of animals; it quietly slips around into the most hidden places and secures its prey with as little danger to itself as possible. Taking the position that Samson, little sun, is a great teacher, who has shown that "he pleased the Lord mightily," as we are continually assured that he did, then what more probable than that he had many students studying under him whom he could send out two by two as he did two thousand years ago, bearing the torch of truth between them, and setting the grain and olive yards (or the followers of materialists and the inner schools), setting them on fire of the spirit, slipping about in their quiet unassuming way. One is reminded of the charge He gave two thousand years ago when He sent the disciples out, "strive with no man."

So these messengers, wise as serpents and harmless as doves, slip about among the people of the materialistic school, and with their torches of truth set on fire the error of the old doctrine, and it was utterly consumed; then in the enthusiasm of their conversion, the Materialists themselves took the new inspiration to the school that had rejected Samson, and burned the school and its promoter with the fire of spirituality, the sacred flame of truth. Then the account goes on to say that he smote them hip and thigh, with a great conquering, or he impressed upon them the necessity of conquering their desire natures. The thigh is ever a symbol of animal desire. Jacob's thigh is withered by the angel before he can give the new name that indicates the Second Great Initiation. Hermes is represented as having a golden thigh. Gold is the symbol of God's righteousness and wisdom.

Samson himself has conquered the animal nature of the new body he is now to handle, and in the rush of the memories of his past existences that the victory probably brought to the Initiate that he was, he is fired by a strong desire to convey the truth to others, and he was evidently successful to a wonderful degree.

From this struggle he retires to the cleft in the rock at Etam. Etam means a high cave in the mountains, probably the cave of Initiation, where he may have taken others if not taking an Initiation himself.

Here in this retirement he is sought out by friends who represent that he must allow them to pretend that they have captured him, in order to take him back to the people who need him too sorely to be deserted now that they are all stirred up. So he consents to pretend to be their prisoner, that he may get the opportunity to get at the people. The "Spirit of the Lord descends upon him mightily" and he takes the moist jawbone of an ass (or the sympathetic common talk of the common people), and smote (converted) a thousand people. We have a survival of this use of jawbone in the usage of the vulgar man when he speaks of "jawing" his wife. The "Kabbalah" says: "Bearing iniquity on the one side and passing over transgressions on the other side is called His Jawbones in Scripture." Here we have the probable text for Samson's discourse.

Then he, the High Initiate, says: "I thirst, shall I die of thirst?" (for the higher wisdom). Must I, an Initiate, spend my time talking these simple truths to the simple-minded people? Then suddenly his eyes are opened and he perceives a stream of wisdom flowing out of that very jawbone he had used, sufficient to assuage even his thirst. The truths he had given out seemed so very obvious, that he wondered that he needed to state them;

yet this second view of them showed him the grand and glorious reality that stood behind those statements of God's love and mercy that mitigates the judgment of man, and his soul is refreshed as he sees that the first day of man's progress is as good in God's eyes as the last.

Translators have had a puzzling time with this passage, for even the most conservative could but perceive the inconsistency in having a Nazerite use a bone from a carcass as a weapon, but to have a stream of water spring up out of the old bone, and he with his vow of purification to drink out of it and yet be mightily assisted by the Lord, presented unsurmountable difficulties; so they assumed that the place where the battle was fought might have resembled a jawbone, in the curve of the hill, and they very considerately caused the water to flow up out of the ground to save Samson's reputation for cleanliness.

But Samson had conquered the body, and its needs would not have caused him to break his vow. The needs of the body do not disturb him. All that he craves is Divine Wisdom, and this he finds can be found in all of its strength and purity just as well in the dealings of the father with the child soul, as with the Initiate. He sees that, as Krishna taught, the Divine Law is perfect no matter upon which plane it may be studied. That the first day of creation is as good in God's eyes as the last.

We find this thirst for Divine Wisdom brought out strongly in the next allegory, Chapter xv of Judges. In this chapter he goes to Gaza, which means strong, a strong center of religious teachings evidently. He goes in unto a harlot. The reader will remember that the word harlot was a common symbol for a school of wisdom that accepted truths from various sources. Evidently Samson wants to study the various systems of religion.

The people of Gaza (strong) say, "Let be till morning light and we will kill him," or wait until he comes into the light of our teachings, and we will conquer him, but at midnight, or long before they supposed possible, he had taken their gates, pulling the posts up out of the ground, and carried them off on his back to Hebron, or the league of great Hierophants. He had appropriated all of the strong points of their philosophy and left them defenceless.

After studying the different philosophies he finds a school in

Sorek. Now Sorek means choice wine; as wine is a symbol of spirituality, we may infer that this school has some method of training the spiritual faculties, the only thing that would have tempted Samson, and from what follows it may be inferred that they taught the negative methods of trance work. In Judges xvi, beginning with the fourth verse, we read: "And it came to pass afterward that he loved a woman in the valley, or by the brook of Sorek. Woman means symbolically Mystery work, brook symbolizes wisdom; so he is interested in the school of wisdom called Delilah.

The meaning of the word Delilah is lost in antiquity, the only meanings given in the dictionaries being those derived from the literal reading of the allegory. It is possible that the Greek word Delphi may have come from the same ancient root primarily. At any rate, that word conveyed to the mind of the ancient at the time of Ezra the idea of the oracle at Delphi, who gave her prophecies in a trance condition. This is a guess, of course, but it looks as though there was some connection between the words as we note that Samson goes to sleep on Delilah's knees. It seems probable that the school taught negative methods of development.

This method, while it opened the Astral Plane to the student, has the danger attendant upon it that the student may be deceived by the illusions of the plane, and may also become obsessed. One may infer from the previous experiences of Samson that he was able to function consciously upon the higher planes, and that he pretended to become unconscious while making his investigations in the Delilah school, but at each attempt to entrap him he showed plainly that it was but a ruse. Being able to function consciously there was no need of trance work, and when he allowed himself to be overcome by the arguments of the school and really went into a trance condition, he, by that act, proved false to his Nazerite vow, and put his eyes out upon the higher planes; that is, he made himself the victim of hypnotism, which interfered with his doing the work in the old positive fashion. But after finding that this method causes him to be the prisoner of the Philistines, or the progressive materialists, he regains his strength by the growth of his hair, or by the renewal of his Nazerite vows, regains his own pure spiritual insight again and easily discriminates between the true and the false. There is a great occult truth hidden in this story, that all who are seeking to unfold along spiritual lines should understand. If one opens up by the cultivation of the soul virtues first, then the consciousness being in touch with the higher planes, is guarded against the errors incident to the Astral Plane; so Samson could not be bound long by Astral illusions for his higher plane consciousness must reveal to him the errors in the methods of Astral trance work. One opening up in the negative way, becomes the slave of some will other than his own. Samson allowed his hair to be shorn; that is, he ignored the true source of his strength, which his hair symbolized, his ability to consciously function upon the different planes, to see what the methods used by the school would bring forth, and he finds that such methods close his eyes upon the higher planes, and not until his hair grows, or his spiritual vibrations are re-established, can he have the strength to assert himself; but when that is done he breaks the pillars upon which the whole structure of their teachings rest, and the negative methods developing the desire nature is conquered or put a stop to, and he demonstrates that he knows the proper methods.

He says, "Let my Soul die with the Philistines." He had killed his animal nature when he killed the lion, he has now conquered the Astral Plane, and in one great struggle he says let my Soul die; that is, he finishes the conquest of the Mental Plane, the Soul is now the vehicle for the God that he is. He is Master of all planes of matter, he has attained the right to go into retirement to serve humanity from the secret places as the Christs ever do, he was buried in the home of peace.

When the physical body of Samson really died we are not told, for the physical body is of little importance in the spiritual reading of the allegories, except as it serves to develop the higher consciousness. In such stories as this, have the Masters hidden the truths, that, as our intuition develops, will be revealed to our astonished gaze, giving us just the hints needed to guide us into the light of true understanding, and enable us to attain the great spiritual strength of Samson, the little sun, our Great Loving Elder Brother, our Christ, today.

Here we have seen the Great One conquer the last of his vehicles that needs to be conquered to make him one of the anointed, or a Messiah. As Jacob he was given the Second Great Initiation, as Aaron he received the third, as Samson he crucifies all, or takes the Fourth Great Initiation. In this life we note he has to pass through all again, or recall the preceding ones. So "Samson pleased God mightily." Is it not plainly to be seen why?

The next incarnation in which we find the great entity whom we call the Christ, is shown in the allegories telling of the doings of David.

Here let me explain that it may be possible that the Jews had, away back in the past some time, a king that they called David, but I fancy he would be extremely astonished to find himself confused with the David that the allegories deal with. Even as our descriptive "Napoleons of finance" would have no meaning had there been no warrior Napoleon who impressed upon the world the fact that he was unique, so there may have been a traditional David about whom the Jew had woven many tales in the course of the ages and this gave to Ezra and his inspirers just the right kind of a story under which to hide the occult knowledge, and at the same time cultivate the patriotism of the race that they were to lead out of slavery. It is very significant to find that Jeshua (Jesus), Noahdiah (Noah the beloved of God), and Moses, Ezra IV, 3, and Eleazar (Master Koot Hoomi), Ezra VII, 33, were Ezra's helpers at this time. What more natural than that they should have rewritten the Books of the Law, as it is stated that they did? That the incidents recorded happened at some date before they were compiled is, of course, certain, but the exact date of any of them cannot be proven. That Ezra lived during a part of the life of the great Buddha, is probable, according to history, and that the great religious enthusiasm of the period must have reached Babylon is equally sure. Ezra was an Initiate, as were many of his associates, Daniel among them. That his nation was freed from their bondage at this time was undoubtedly due to the great events that had revolutionized the religious thought of the day. What more natural than that they should have woven some of these events into their new Book of the Law that was to furnish the Scripture of the new fifth root race, and give to the new people the true Mystery teaching, hidden in these stories, giving them a record that they would eventually find complete when they arrive at the point of evolution sufficient to comprehend the full meaning.

The King David stories seem to date from this period. But, says some one, you do not mean to say you are putting King David in the same age as the Buddha, when David lived about 1000 B. C. and the Buddha only between 562 and 482 approximately? I answer, an allegory illustrating a truth is a different thing from literal history, although usually based upon historic occurrences may be transferred to any age. However, from the symbolic reading of these allegories the teaching seems to be that this David really did live at the same time that Buddha did, and that he was the same entity that we now call the Christ.

Paul testifies to the truth of this in Hebrews x, 5:

"Wherefore when He (Christ) cometh into the world, he saith,
Sacrifice and offering thou wouldst not,
But a body didst thou prepare for me;
In whole burnt offerings and sacrifice for sin thou hadst no pleasure;
Then I said, Lo I come to do Thy will, O God.
In the roll of the book it written of me."

The translators all seem to agree that this XL Psalm was written by David, and Paul is speaking of Christ when he says: "When he cometh into the world He saith this."

Many traces of the Aryan origin of these stories still cling to them in spite of the Hebrew coloring that has been given them, and if one gets the full magnitude of the scheme of man's evolution, it will make no difference whether the incidents recorded took place in India or in Palestine. The important thing is to get at the truths they teach, and get a clear understanding of the great good law, at once the most perfect, the most just, the most soul satisfying that it is possible to conceive.

Let us take a moment considering the meaning of the symbols used to bring the David stories before us. Saul (symbol of the established religion of that day), of the tribe of Benjamin, "the wolf that raveneth," the church that swallows everything that comes near it. You will see later on how it tries to swallow, or appropriate, the heroic deeds of Jonathan, and tries to swallow David by putting him in charge of the Mystery work; the wolf that raveneth is surely a fitting name. Saul is introduced to us as hunting his father's asses, or looking after the common people who have strayed from the church fold. "He stands head and shoulders above his brethren," by far the most promising religious movement of the age; and Samuel the Great Initiator, thinks that by giving the old church a new spiritual impulse that it may do to start the new fifth root race upon its career. So Saul is taken to the mount of spirituality when he is anxious over his father's lost asses (common people), and Samuel sets before him the choicest spiritual viands he has, to fortify him for the new work. Soon, however, Saul demonstrates that he is unfit for the work. He is helpless in the presence of the giant materialism that assails him on every hand. He finds that his materialistic armor is not proof against Goliath, and David throws it aside when it is handed to him. Saul also shows a lack of obedience and reverence in presumptuously daring to take the place of Samuel. Here again we see that desire to swallow everything, he will usurp even the place of the Great Initiator. He does not understand the true ideal of the fifth root race. To him the great ideal of a religion is power.

How different is David. He is found caring for his father's sheep (the fifth race people) on the spiritual hillsides. He is fearless because of his perfect confidence in God, and because he has slain his lion (conquered his stars—in this incarnation he was born under Leo), and killed his bear (his animal nature). He has no use for Saul's material armor, so he picks up a few stones from the brook of wisdom, and throws them with the simple directness of a teacher (the shepherd's sling), and the great giant falls face downward. Materialism is conquered by a pebble of God's truth, for it sinks into the forehead, or the comprehension, and then David takes Goliath's own sword, or his own arguments, the truths he has himself perceived to complete the victory. Thus does illumination come from the true wisdom of God, penetrating to the understanding when material considerations are left entirely out of sight. The giant materialism falls powerless when he sees the truth and perceives the scientific facts fall into their natural places.

The people are quick to see the superiority of David, and sing "Saul has slain his thousands, and David his ten thousands." This arouses the jealousy of Saul (the established church), and

ARE THESE SOME INCARNATIONS OF OUR BLESSED CHRIST?

he at once sees the necessity of swallowing this promising youth, so Michael, the daughter, or the inner Mystery work, is given to David, that, as Saul is represented to say, "she may be a snare to him"; that is, keep him busy in the regular church.

Remember, David came through the line of Jesse (wealthy). He came through the line of the spiritually wealthy, of the tribe of Ephraim, the son of Joseph, whom Jacob blessed with the words, "Thee will all Israel bless, and will pray God make thee as Ephraim and Mannassah; and he places Ephraim first." So the line is unbroken from Israel himself through the psychic son of Rachel (Master K. H.).

He makes strenuous efforts to restore the Ark of the Covenant to the people, to get them to appreciate the value of striving to attain the perfect ideal, but his first efforts end disastrously because of the lack of purity of the ones he is training (they reach out impure hands to steady the Ark of the Covenant, the symbol of the perfect man, and are killed by the vibrations of purity emanating from that marvelous symbol). This puts a check upon his enthusiasm for awhile, for he fears that it is too soon to expect so much. Later on, when the Ark is about to really be restored to Israel again, he dances naked, that is, naked of bodies, or naked of earthly possessions. Certain Initiates were called the naked, because they renounced all worldly possessions. David probably danced naked of bodies, that is, in spirit. He danced at the thought of the true ideal being restored to the people. But his wife, Saul's daughter, despises him in her heart, because of this attitude, for it meant that he intended to admit to the Mysteries all who were ready, instead of admitting only the privileged few, as the conservative old church had settled down to doing. When she protests he tells her he will still further debase himself before the Lord; that is, he will humble himself to any extent for the good of the people. We are told that Michael had no children from that day. The old Mystery work was too set in its prejudices to meet with the demands made necessary by the advance of the new race; therefore no Initiates came from the old school from that day, the crown had been placed upon David's head, and his school was to develop the ideal of the fifth root race up to its highest standard.

All will remember the cruel tests to which Saul subjected

David, chasing him from pillar to post, from cave to cave, ever striving to kill him, and how David often had an opportunity to kill Saul, but ever resisted the temptation to lay hand upon the Lord's anointed. The reader will also remember how David tried to charm away the evil spirit of Saul by making sweet music for him, or by trying to harmonize his new methods with the old dogmas, trying ever to harmonize, never to antagonize; but the old religion would have none of it. Saul ever tried to kill David. The old church would not change, would not progress.

That I am right in assuming that the established church is symbolized by the character of Saul, is accidentally testified by the statement of the translators themselves in I Sam. xiii, 1. It says: "Saul was years old when he began to reign," and in the margin we are told that, as no number of years were given in the original, the translators inserted the number forty, as that was a probable age for a man to assume the crown. But suppose we assume that this is a mystical history of the fifth root race, and read it as written: "Saul was years old when he began to reign," or the established church was ages old when it began to reign over the fifth root race people, and when he had reigned two years, or through the first two sub races of the fifth root race, he chose three thousand men of Israel (the spiritually minded ones of the new race), whereof two thousand were with Saul in Michmash (or treasure house of spiritual things), and in Mount Bethel (mount, spiritual elevation; Bethel, Temple of God). So these favored ones were on the spiritual heights in the Temple of God, and the others were dwelling in the treasure house of spiritual things. Two thousand were with Saul, and the other thousand were with Jonathan in Gibeah, or on the spiritual heights of Benjamin (the wolf that raveneth, or swallows everything she can get—the religion that takes in all new truths and makes it a part of itself if possible). Jonathan, the eldest son, the prince of the ancient church, was the one whom we know as the Buddha, whom the Bible mentions in another place as Melchizedek. With this majestic personage, upon the spiritual heights of the ancient religion of the fourth root race, the perfect example of what it might produce, did it but stay faithful to its early teachings; were a thousand of the highly evolved of the new fifth root race. Could the old church only live up to the ideal of her founder, there would be no need of any interference, but the church as a whole cannot rise to the altitude of its noblest son, and he recognizes the necessity of breaking up the old form which has become too crystallized to be useful to train the new race. This is one of the religions that he himself helped to found in the past ages, but he is here now to help start a new impulse to quicken religious growth.

How beautifully the characteristics of the old church are brought out, keeping up the reputation of the wolf that raveneth. Jonathan with his thousand devoted spiritual followers, conquers the materialism of Geba, and they make a great reputation among the Philistines; so Saul blew the trumpet throughout the land, saying, let the people hear, and all Israel heard that *Saul* had smitten the garrison at Geba Thus did the old church swallow up the Buddha and his fifth root race followers, calling the victories his, although they were gained by methods exactly the reverse of those he practiced. Thus does he gratify his desire.

David is chased from cave to cave; from caves of Initiation or spiritual retreats, where the malice of the old church drives him to seek refuge; and he draws about him all those who are dissatisfied with the existing order of things, all who are sufficiently evolved to understand him.

The women spoken of are schools of Mystery work that he taught the true methods of development Those who accept the truth in its fullness are spoken of as wives. They bring to him presents of bread and wine, or such physical and spiritual gifts as they have to offer, and in return he takes them into his heart, and teaches them the greater Mysteries, giving them the spiritual baptism that makes them one with him

The names prove that these women are not women at all: Michael means "who is like unto God," Abigail means "father of exaltation" (not even in the feminine gender), Ahinoam means "brother of exaltation."

Nabal (foolish) is evidently the exoteric work of a certain locality which rejects the overtures of David, but the inner Mystery work recognizes the authority of the Great One and offers him hospitality. Later Abigail (father of exaltation) becomes his wife, or his favorite group of Mystery workers.

Let us take a little notice of the story of Bath-Sheba (daughter of an oath is the meaning of the word). Uriah means "my light is Lord Jehovah"; this locates the work represented. It is the religious work of the Hittites. Uriah is the exoteric church, and Bath-Sheba the inner or Mystery work. David is upon the housetop, or is working upon the upper planes, when his notice is attracted by the careful purifying process that the school of Bath-Sheba is teaching. You remember he sees her bathing in the fountain (of wisdom) and is much pleased with her appearance. Why? Because he saw that they were really purifying their subtile bodies and were very earnest in their desire to become perfect. So he sends for them and lies with them, or teaches them the full Mystery work, until they are one with him (wives symbolically. We have an echo of this use of the word lie in our "lay to it" to indicate persevering effort. So well do they receive the teaching that an Initiate (child) is born very soon. Uriah, the exoteric workers come, and David tells them to go to their own inner work and purify themselves, "Go to his house and wash his feet"; but their idea is, that in fidelity rather than purification lies their chance for growth, and they refuse to leave the king's door. Seeing this devotion, David does reward them; he invites them in to the kitchen, the only plane of consciousness that they can function on, and makes them drunken (spiritually), then sends them out in the thick of the controversial fight between the fifth race exponents of doctrine and the Ammonites (possibly these Ammonites were the Egyptian school, who called their god Ammon Ra, or they may have been Lot's descendents), the spiritual-mountaineers of the fourth root race, hoping that they will be conquered (convinced), and they are.

David makes Bath-Sheba his wife, or his favorite band of Mystery workers, placing them at the head of all the schools along that line. But the Lord Jehovah objects. Why? Because the Lord Jehovah is looking after the natural evolution of each race, and for the more advanced fifth root race to take up a fourth root race work and give it this prominence, while it may be good for the Hittites, is certainly somewhat of a hindrance to the fifth race, for the Hittite must of necessity drag somewhat because of immaturity. David, while admitting that he has sinned against evolution or against the physical law, yet because of the great love he bears the lower race, fasts and tries everything in his power to make the child that is born of the union live; but the Hittite nature is too little evolved to stand the strain of the drastic measures of the higher work, and the first Initiate dies.

As Jacob, David has supplanted Esau, getting the blessing that really belonged to the elder brother; as David, he returns the blessing, by favoring Bath-Sheba and giving the race of Esau the first and strongest support in their mystery work. Thus is the ancient debt paid. Thus also is his vow to Jonathan kept.

The second Initiate is Solomon (harmony), renamed by Lord Jehovah, Jedidiah (beloved by Jehovah). So from the great love of the Messiah of the fifth root race, is the impulse given to give all of the races the same opportunity to attain, and from this union of races is born the Great One who is to be the Messiah of the sixth root race, Solomon, Master Koot Hoomi. David, the Christ of the fifth root race, in his great love, unites the races in a great bond of brotherly love, and will through the ages gather the living stones, or the perfected humans (Masters), supply the mortar of universal love, and the "pillars that go no more out"; and Solomon (harmony, beloved of God) will fashion this material gathered by David into the great Temple of the living God, eternal in the heavens, which shall be completed in seven years, or seven races, when will come the Great Rest Day, the millennium, or the pralaya of the Hindoo.

Let us look for a moment at the so-called sons of David: The meaning of the word Absolom is "my father is peace," and indicates who David is, the Prince of Peace.

To understand the story of Absolom it is necessary to consider the condition of things that faced David in that incarnation. All of the systems of religions taught in their Mysteries the descent of Spirit into matter and the means by which it was to gain its freedown from the thraldom of the flesh. In those early days of the race the physical was much more vigorous than it is today, and, naturally, the struggle to subdue the physical propensities was much fiercer than anything we know of. In the course of ages the reason for the struggle became lost, to a great extent in the intensity of the struggle itself, and man forgot that he was being taught this secret to enable him to assist his brother to attain also, so intent was he upon his own struggle. In order to accomplish this with as little distraction as possible, he retired into monasteries in remote places away from the temptations of ordinary life. David (Christ), then, as later, taught the Mysteries, but taught men that the development was to enable them to assist their brothers, and that in loving service the same effects might be attained in regard to self control and purifying the subtile bodies, as by ascetic discipline. He has ever taught the Gospel of Love. Though he taught the disciples in the house and warned them not to cast their pearls before swine, yet he sent them out to preach the good news according to what the people were able to stand. The conservative teachings of all old religions after the crystallizing process has begun has always been "Come ye out from among them," but the great loving heart of the Master ever has taught "Go ye out among them."

In the David incarnation the Master was a warrior for God, or an aggressive exponent of truth, striving ever to correct error, seeking ever to serve the people, and sending out such strong love vibrations that his people often speak of him as being "like unto an angel of God."

When Absolom tries to wrench the kingdom from him by violence, he will not strive with him, but flies from him. Absolom is trying to gain the kingdom of his father, which is the Christ consciousness, but he consults with others rather than David, and is advised to go in unto his father's concubines, that is, study in the schools that have only partially accepted David's views, rather than study under David himself. Unselfish service does not attract, if he can attain some other way. David is greatly pained by this attitude of Absolom, as he knows that what he seeks can be gained only through the path of love, and he realizes how great a teacher Absolom would make would he but be guided aright. Absolom, therefore, would take the kingdom of heaven by violence, or by certain practices that were taught in some of the schools, rather than by devoting himself in unselfish service to others, and the Great Prince of Peace flies from him in grief, for not to such methods can the real Christ consciousness respond. Absolom traveling through the forest of Ephraim (among the teachers of another school), on the spiritual hilltops where he was fighting his battle, gets his hair tangled in the boughs of a great oak. It will be remembered that we found that a great oak is a symbol of a strong teacher, and that long hair was the sign of a Nazerite, in this case probably a Nazerite of days. Absolom had probably taken the Nazerite vow not to cut his hair until he found what he was after. After he has caught his hair or has given his Nazerite vow of fidelity to the great teacher of this other school, and submits to its discipline, then his mule (his animal nature) left him, and then it was that the arrows of truth shot by the leader of his father's forces pierce him to the heart; but now it is too late. He is by his vow buried under the Stones (Masters) of Ephraim. That is, he is vowed to the inner work of a conservative school. And David grieves at the loss of such a strong, vigorous teacher as Absolom would have made to have strengthened the new impulse that he was trying to give the religious teachings of the day. Absolom is pictured as being greatly beloved by the common people, consequently his power would have been great.

Adonijah, another son of David, is pictured as trying to get the kingdom of his father. Adonijah is the Hebrew for Adonis. The meaning is "my Lord is Jehovah," significant when we remember that Adonis was a god of nature, and at this time he was one of the most popular gods of the Orient. He is represented in the allegories as endeavoring to win the whole race by his sweet and winsome ways, and is pictured as inviting all of the most prominent men to a feast in order to gain their support to his cause. This is told to David by Bath-Sheba, the school of wisdom that he had won from the Hittites, from which union is born Solomon (Jedidiah, Harmony, beloved of God), to whom the kingdom has been promised by David.

When David hears that Adonijah aspires to the universal kingdom, or being the spiritual king over all of the nations, he proclaims that to Solomon alone has that succession been given. Solomon (Master Koot Hoomi) is to succeed himself as Messiah. You will remember that Solomon's first prayer is for wisdom, and he is told that because he asked for that he shall have all things. By wisdom, born of harmony, beloved of God, will be built the great Temple of the living God. When Solomon is proclaimed the Great King, Adonijah is frightened and grasps the horns of the altar for protection, but wisdom begotten of harmony of all creeds is now the ruler, and Solomon simply sends him home with the injunction to sin not; that is, he is to do his work upon his own plane, and do it as well as he can. Wisdom recognizes the rights of all, and would force none. Each of the branches of the religious work has its place, Solomon only stipulates that he shall give out true teachings. So wisdom, begotten from harmony, beloved of God, starts the building of the great Temple of the Living God eternal in the heavens, in which it is destined that each of us will be placed as living stones hewn and polished at the quarry and ready to be placed where we belong without sound of hammer. And some of us may be pillars that will go no more out. We have not the space to handle the rest of the sons, but this will suffice to show the allegorial trend of the story.

But to go back to David. We see him in sweetness and patience bidding God's time; while Saul does as he will; knowing that he has received the anointing that makes him the spiritual king of the new root race, yet nevertheless submitting to the most humiliating experiences, and in no way trying to push himself into notice or claiming his right to the throne.

In I Sam. XVIII we are told that when David had ceased telling who he was, that the soul of Jonathan was knit with the soul of David, and he loved him as his own soul. This story, no matter from what plane it has been read, has given to the world one of the most beautiful and inspiring conceptions of the possibilities of love between man and man that can be found in literature. That this exquisite example should have been set the race by the two Great Masters of Love and Compassion, the great spiritual leaders of the fourth and fifth root races, seems most fitting. Who could so well show forth the true spirit of love and devotion.

Before we go farther perhaps we had better stop long enough to show our grounds for the assumption that Jonathan is the incarnation of the one whom we call Gautama Buddha.

In "Inner Life," Mr. Leadbeater tells us that, "When our planet reached the place where it should provide a Buddha from the fruits of its own humanity, no one was found competent to fill the place."

"Two Great Ones stood together at the head of the race, at the level of the Bodhisattva (Messiah) degree Gautama Buddha, the Bodhisattva (Messiah) of the fourth root race, and Lord Maitreya, or the one whom we call the Christ. Gautama, because of his great love for humanity, decided to take the tremendous tests necessary to qualify him for the position, and gave the position of Messiah to our Christ, whom he dearly loved. This happened in the incarnation in which we know him as Gautama.

With these facts in mind, let us see what we find in the XIV chapter of I Sam. It says: "Now it fell upon a day that Jonathan, the son of Saul, said unto his armor-bearer (his heart), come let us go over to the Philistine garrison, that is on yonder side." Philistine means emigrants, or travelers, so the suggestion is, let us go over to the stronghold of those who are on the other side, as regards attainment, and undertake the conquest of the spiritual truths needed to establish myself.

He was not expected to do this, for "he told not his father," Saul, and the third verse states that "the people knew not that Jonathan was gone." Now come the tests:

4th verse: "And between the passes by which Jonathan sought to go over unto the Philistine garrison, there was a rocky crag on the one side, and a rocky crag on the other side, and the name of one was Bozez, and the name of the other was Senah. The one crag rose on the north in front of Michmash" (house of treasure) "and the other crag rose in front of Geba" (spiritual elevation).

There is a significance in these crags, rocks they are, "established in strength." Bozez means this very thing, and Senah means thorny strength. To realize the full significance one needs to recall the symbolism of the Temple of Solomon. The reader will remember that upon each side of the door of the inner sanctuary was a pillar, one named Boaz, and one named Jachim, the meaning of these two words being exactly the same as Bozez and Senah. In the ritual of the temple the priest came out of his cell on the north, symbolic of the physical, and another came from a cell on the south of the door, or the spiritual, and the two entered together through the east door, symbolic of the intellect, on their journey toward the west, where the Ark of God, or the symbol of the perfect man, sat. Do you not grasp the symbolism? The physical, desire nature, and the spiritual must join hands, and enter through the door of intelligent comprehension of law to attain perfection. And they must pass between the two great forces established in strength, the Priest, Great White Force, and

Patriarch, the Great Black Force, or the positive and negative forces, one tending to discouragement, because of its thorns.

"So Jonathan said to his armor-bearer" (his heart) "let us show ourselves" (that is, show my willingness), "and it may be that the Lord will work for us." "Then Jonathan said, behold we will pass over and disclose ourselves unto the men, and if they say unto us tarry, until we come to you, then will we stand in our place, and not go up unto them." He will see if the Great ones think he can accomplish the feat, and then do as he is directed, sure of the help of God in either case. "But if they say to us come up to us, then will we go up, for the Lord hath delivered them into our hand; and this shall be a sign unto us."

So he showed himself and received the invitation to make the effort, and he said "the Lord hath delivered them into the hand of Israel" (the prince that prevails with God). And Jonathan climbs up upon his hands and feet, a steep hard climb, and conquered every obstacle, and there was great slaughter, or a great victory, and no one could stand before him. His spiritual strength was overwhelming. In Verse 15 we are told that "there was a great trembling in the camp, and in the field, and among all the people; even the earth quaked, so there was an exceeding great trembling. And the multitude melted away." His enemies disappeared.

Now Saul, the established church, begins to see that something has happened. The enemies of spirituality have been put to rout. Who has done this thing? He has his people numbered to see who is missing, and it is discovered that Jonathan alone is absent. Saul calls for the Ark to be brought, and consults the ancient symbol, while Jonathan the reality, the man perfected, wins the victory by living the life, causing the enemy to fight among themselves, defeating their own cause. Farther on we are told that the men of Israel, the highly evolved fifth root race men, who had been hiding in the hill country of Ephraim, or on the spiritual heights, came out and helped in the struggle. "So the Lord saved Israel" (the prince that prevails with God) "that day," while the old church was bowing before the ancient symbol of what had now actually come into existence, without realizing at all the significance of what was happening.

Verse 24 reads: "And the men of Israel were distressed that

day, for Saul had adjured the people saying, cursed be the man that eateth anything until I be avenged upon my enemies " After the ancient usage he calls for a fast, and his followers all obey, but Jonathan not knowing of the command takes some honey and eats of it. Read I Sam. xiv from the 27th verse. I have not the time to enter into it, but surely here is an allegory showing that he stood for doing away with unnecessary punishment of the body, even as the Buddha did. The ancient church would have put him to death but the love of the people protected him.

Jonathan takes the honey upon the rod in his hand, the rod of Initiation, and at once he experiences illumination, and realizes that the fast, weakening the physical, prevents the best work, and he thus expresses himself. That he was right is shown by the fact that as soon as the restriction is lifted the people in their haste to supply their necessities eat the animals killed in their blood, a great sin in the eyes of the ancients. Thus it is demonstrated that enforced fasts cause the people to sin.

When David returned from slaying the great giant of materialism with a pebble of God's wisdom, Saul asked him who he was, and he answered that he was the son of Jesse (wealthy, great spiritual possessions) the Bethlehemite (or from the house of bread, or the Temple of God). To put it more plainly, he had come through a line of great spirituality directly from the temple service of the ages.

I Sam. 18: "And it came to pass, when he had made an end to speaking unto Saul, that the soul of Jonathan was knit with the soul of David. And Jonathan loved him as his own soul, and Saul took him that day and would let him go no more home to his father's house" (swallowed him).

3. "Then Jonathan and David made a covenant, because he loved him as his own soul."

4. "And Jonathan stripped himself of the robe that was upon him, and gave it to David, and his apparel, even to his sword, to his bow, and to his girdle"; that is, he turned over to David all of his ensignia of rank as Messiah.

5. "And David went out whithersoever Saul sent him" (worked patiently in the established church), "and behaved himself wisely; and Saul set him over the men of war" (gave him

the aggressive spiritual work to do), "and it pleased all of the people."

15. "When Saul saw that he behaved himself wisely he stood in awe of him."

16. "But all Israel" (fifth root race people, who were spiritually minded), "and Judah" (the Jews) "loved David."

David has a hard time, being chased from pillar to post by the narrow conservatism of the established religion, but in spite of the persecution he gathers quite a band about him, and has two schools of inner work that he has been able to educate in the greater Mysteries, which he calls wives. Many times he has an opportunity to stretch forth his hand and take the kingdom from Saul, but always does he refrain from asserting himself, waiting the time of the Great Ones. His character is attested by the words of Achish in I Sam., Chapter XXIX, Verse 9: "I know thou art good as an angel of God." His treatment of Shimei, after his reviling him, as he was fleeing from Absolom, shows that his policy was ever one of forgiveness, where the individual was concerned, but in handling the great errors of metaphysical reasoning, he "slew" or conquered hosts of enemies. The battles fought by David were bloodless; they were battles of brain rather than brawn, of spirit rather than flesh. He was the great warrior of the Lord, fighting to establish the true Mysteries again upon the earth; going from one ancient school to another, trying to purge them of the errors that had crept into them.

We find that David took the throne only upon the death of Jonathan, which agrees exactly with the Hindoo account of the transfer of the Bodhisattvic, or Messianic, position to Lord Maitreya (our Christ). In II Sam. I we find a very beautiful tribute to Jonathan and the old religion, or Saul.

"Thy Gazell, O Israel, is slain upon thy high places"; that is, thy swift traveling one (Buddha) is conquered by thy high spiritual possibilities.

"How are the mighty fallen" (conquered).

"Tell it not in Gath" (the capitol of the Philistines, or progressive materialism).

"Publish it not in Ashkelon" (stronghold of black art),

"Lest the daughters of the Philistines rejoice" (not understanding),

"Lest the daughters of the uncircumcised" (the impure) "triumph."

"Saul and Jonathan were lovely and pleasant in their lives,"

"And in their death they were not divided,"

"They were swifter than the eagles" (eagles fly swifter and higher than any other bird),

"They were stronger than the lion."

"Ye daughters of Israel" (Aryan or fifth root race)

"Weep over Saul" (pay proper respect for the old religion, although you are getting more advanced ideas), "for"

"She clothed you with scarlet delicately" (she looked lovingly after your needs up to this time).

"Who put ornaments of gold upon your apparel" (gold means righteousness, wisdom).

"How are the mighty conquered, in the midst of battle" (or struggle).

"Jonathan is conquered upon thy high places" (Planes of high spirituality).

"I am distressed for thee, my brother Jonathan" (he misses his personal presence),

"Very pleasant hast thou been unto me,
Thy love to me was wonderful,
Passing the love of woman.
How are the mighty conquered,
And the weapons of war perished." (The arguments of the old order of things are so weakened that they have lost their power before the higher ideals that have now become established.)

David, however, is not yet to have peace, for old abuses are strongly entrenched although the Buddha's teachings have done much to assist him; yet this entire incarnation is one of ceaseless struggle against wrong ideas of how to gain the higher consciousness, or the kingdom. David is working not only with Jews remember, but with the fifth root race, or the Ayran race. He is a mighty warrior before the Lord, but, as said before, you may rest assured that this David never shed one drop of human or any other blood; the battles he fought were all of them spiritual and intellectual. It was the true mysticism fighting against crystallized dogma and priest-craft. The cold, calculating, self-centered, unsympathetic, unapproachable æsthetic, who considered the whole object of life to be the purifying of the vehicles for the purpose of attaining the higher consciousness for the advancement of self, must be made to realize that this training was of use only as it made of man a tender-hearted sympathizing elder brother ready to extend a helping hand to the younger brethren. So David taught, even as he did in his later incarnation, that by loving service will the purification and the higher consciousness be developed through the universal love vibration, more quickly than by all the mortification of the body that can be practiced. Flesh must be conquered by Spirit, true; but the quicker and more perfect way is by forgetting self in loving service of others. The bodily control is just as truly achieved by this course, and the Buddhic faculties more surely built up, and he becomes a sweet magnetic force for real good in the world.

David, it will be remembered, ate the shew bread in the temple, symbolic of the fact that he should henceforth stand before God continually as High Priest for the people, an "High Priest forever after the order of Melchizedek" (Buddha). Who but Christ occupies this place?

In Amos ix, 9: "For lo I will command, and I will sift the House of Israel" (the fifth root race) "among all nations, like as grain is sifted, yet shall not the least kernel fall to the earth" (none shall be lost). "All the sinners of My people shall die" (be conquered) "by the sword" (by truth) "who say the evil shall not overtake us, or meet us" (who deny that an effect follows a cause, or the law of just compensation, called by the Hindoo "Karma").

II. "In that day will I raise up the tabernacle" (body) "of David that is fallen, and close up the breaches thereof" (all of His vehicles will be connected to the physical again), "and I will build it as in the days of old" (He will be in the flesh among us as of old), "and they shall possess the remnant of Edom and all the nations that are called by my name, saith Jehovah that doeth this. Behold the day shall come, saith Jehovah, that the plowman shall overtake the reaper, and the treader of grapes him that soweth the seed." That is, Christ will again come among us, and under this impulse the younger races will catch up with the older ones, and all shall dwell together in harmony in the promised land of extended consciousness; that is the birthright of the whole of humanity. And David, the King, shall rule, and shall gather the material for the temple, and Solomon, Harmony, beloved of God, shall build the Temple of the Living God without the sound of a hammer or tool or any such thing. The Temple of the Living God, in which each of us may be a stone, bound together by the mortar of the universal love of the Christ within, that the Christ without has taught us to develop.

So we see the same dominant note in Jacob, the first Patriarch of the race; in Aaron, the first High Priest for the fifth root race; in Samson, the first great Judge; and in David, the first great King, that we find in the great Master of Compassion that used the body of Jesus two thousand years ago. The same great unselfish love, the same sweet and gentle compassion, the same unselfish service of others, the same unusual wisdom, the same simple, grandly heroic character going about among men only to do them good. Truly no other character in history can claim these virtues to the same degree as this One Great Ego.

Mr. Leadbeater tells us that he finds "Surya" (our Christ) thirty thousand years ago on the akasic records, and at that remote period He was even then teaching His doctrine of universal love. Two thousand years ago He came to definitely inculcate this teaching in His religious work, and mankind has slowly learned a very small part of the lesson. Some few of us have learned the meaning of unselfish love in connection with our own; possibly in some few cases we may be able to extend it even to our neighbors, but few, very few, know what true universal love means. We have learned the lesson of the lower love; it remains for us to get the conception of the higher love, the love that animates Him. Oh, the magnitude of the conception, the grandeur of the destiny! Truly, as Jeremiah says, "Jacob is the former of all things, and Israel" (the regenerate of the race) "is the tribe of His inheritance: Jehovah of Hosts" (the God in the heart of each man) "is his name." Jer. 51-19; also Jer. 10-16.

As we gain this conception of our at-one-ment with all, then will the teachings of the dear Elder Brother be understood, and we will enter into our inheritance of the promised land of extended consciousness, that will include all planes, and the power that will be ours by right of the victories won, by right of our Sonship with the Eternal Christ our Great Elder Brother, we the many brethern, are all sons of the same Living God, Eternal in the heavens.

He will come again, we are told, "in clouds" (of suspicion) "and great glory" (which will be seen only by the psychic, however). Only as we have developed the Christ vibration in our own souls, will we be able to recognize Him when He does come, for be sure, beloved, in the hour that ye least expect will He appear, and unless we have our lamps trimmed and burning we shall not see who the Great One is, that passes by. Watch, beloved, for the day is at hand, and remember that always before He has appeared in the form of some oppressed people. Watch, I say unto you, WATCH, for the day is at hand.

CHAPTER XII.

THE VISIONS OF EZEKIEL.

As we glance back into the dim mysteries of the past we are often startled to see a brilliant star shining against the dark background, and almost invariably we find that he who sends forth this unusually strong radiance has the reputation of having been either a seer, a prophet, or perhaps both. We note that the tendency of man in all ages has been to bow in awe before supernatural gifts, so much so that the oracles of the different religious systems controlled the affairs of the nations. Kings were crowned or deposed, nations rose or fell as the oracle dictated, and individuals frequently were guided in all of their dealings by the prophecies of the local oracle.

We are inclined to indulge in a smile at this, and attribute it all to pure superstition, but, if as Occultists tell us, great souls came from Venus in such guise to instruct infant humanity at one time, then such a state of things is understandable, and it helps us to fathom the reverence of the Oriental to this day for the dirty holy man that tempts the Westerner to kick him into the sea for a much-needed bath. It is a psychological fact, that the human mind is incapable of originating anything, and receives only what he perceives from experience, or brings through from the higher planes, building after the pattern given him in the Mount (or the higher planes), and this reverence must be the outgrowth of some racial memory. That this memory dealt with facts can hardly be denied, for error dies before long. The sacred books of the earth have come from the hands of individuals, that, in their own age, have impressed the world with their unusual psychic powers, and their real unselfish devotion to the welfare of humanity, and these messages have provided man with food for thought during the ages. To be sure we read of sporadic cases of the lower plane medium making a temporary sensation, yet, as in our own time, such manifestations make no permanent impression upon the race. The records that have stood the test of time, are those that have come from the higher planes, and because of their origin they appeal to the higher nature of man in a way not to be misunderstood.

In Ezekiel we have visions given at various times during a period of twenty-two years. We note, Chapter I, 1, "Now it came to pass in the thirtieth year, in the fourth month, and the fifth day of the month," that thirty, the spiritual triangle, has been added to the quaternary, the physical, and it takes place in the fifth race. It will be remembered that the triangle stands for the perfect spiritual development, when topping a quaternary, or the perfected physical.

Ezekiel seems to have been one of the captives of Babylon and was stationed on the river Chebar. Whether the bondage was a real physical experience or a symbolic one, the reader may decide for himself. Babylon means "Gate of God," and Chebar means "long," so symbolically it may mean that he was resting beside the long river of wisdom that flows by the Gate of God.

He was a priest of Judah, or of the Jews, and one cannot help wondering whether he understood what he wrote, or whether, like Daniel, he would have exclaimed, "I wrote but I understood not."

As I turn the pages of these allegories, I feel that there are depths of meaning that I am not sounding, strains of music too delicate for my ears as yet, and I hand you my conceptions in all humility, simplying saying: "It looks so to me." If you explore you may open vistas that will rival mine as the diamond outshines the quartz crystal in brilliancy; but such as I have I give you. To me it is grand, mysterious, a wonderful testimony of the Master's goodness, that I see so much as I do. As all Scripture has seven distinct meanings suited to guide man upon each of his seven planes of development, it is good for us to use our intuition to discover as much as we can of this hidden meaning. In this way alone will we develop the most wonderful of the faculties that the Trinity has placed in our kingdom.

Let us begin at the eighth Chapter of Ezekiel. Ezekiel sat in his house on the brook, Chebar (long), and the elders of Judah, or the most evolved egos of the Jews, were with him. Ezekiel was a priest of Judah, but you notice that it is not the priests that are with him when he gets into a sufficiently high vibration to get a vision of the higher planes, but the most highly evolved of the tribes, the elders. He was taken to the Temple in Jerusalem (peace) by the Lord Jehovah, who is not only the Lord of the Physical Plane but also acts often as Great Initiator.

The Jews were a people chosen of Lord Jehovah to act as the priestly caste, and they are given the care of the oracles of God, as St. Paul tells us. They were not Israel, but they were Israel's sister, and they had been false to their trust; they had rebelled against the Lord Jehovah, they were stiff-necked.

Now note the vision: "Son of man, lift up thine eyes. And I lifted up mine eyes, and behold northward of the altar, an image of jealousy." The "North" gate of the Temple, symbolic of the physical, controlled by jealousy. In Verse 14 we find the women sitting by this same gate "Weeping for Tammuz." Tammuz originally a god symbolizing the Second Logos manifesting in the flesh, but at this time greatly degraded by phallic conceptions of the people, and worshipped by rites of feasting and physical gratification, was tempting the motherhood of the people to turn from the north gate intended only for the entrance of consecrated physical nature, while within the Temple itself stood a huge image of jealousy, blocking the way even though they should turn that way. Truly a sad picture of the carnal desires of the race.

"Son of man, seest thou what they do, even the great abominations that the House of Israel do?" Remember the House of Israel means the fifth root race, not the Jews. The Jews are spoken of as Judah.

Jerusalem means "peace," and the Temple is symbolic of the spiritual consciousness of humanity. Take the larger view of this vision and you will perceive that it applies full as well to our own time as it did to those more ancient days. Do we not find jealousy and sensuality shutting people out of the higher planes of consciousness?

"And he brought me to the door of the court, and when I looked behold a hole in the wall, and he said, Son of man dig now in the wall, and when I had digged in the wall" (wall symbolizes the extent of the consciousness of the individual or race), "behold a door. And he said unto me, Go in and see the wicked abominations that they do here, and I went in and saw all sorts of creeping things, and all sorts of idols of the House of Israel, and the elders of the House of Israel." Remember the elders of the House of Judah were sitting with him while he was seeing this vision, and for that reason may infer that they were not of this sort. So in this hidden room (the inner consciousness of the race) he saw all of this sensuality and materialism, and found that they were led in their depravity by their elders, those who should have been their spiritual leaders. Here they all were offering incense (worshipping) the idols of their own imagining.

"Then he said to me, Son of man, hast thou seen what the elders of the House of Israel do in the dark, every man in his chambers of imagery? for they say there is no Jehovah (Jehovah of Hosts, the God in the heart of man). "Jehovah hath deserted the Land" (the inner consciousness).

Have not many of our own people lost the idea of God within and of Justice, forgetting the great law of compensation, and upholding the substitutionary nature of the sacrifice of Christ, in spite of His Own words, "With what measure ye mete it shall be measured to you again," and St. Paul's "Be not deceived, God is not mocked; whatsoever a man soweth, that shall he also reap"?

Certainly they are worshipping idols of their own imagining.

"He said, 'Thou shalt see yet other great abominations that they do.' And he brought me to the inner Court of the Lord's House, and behold, at the door of the Temple of the Lord, between the porch and the altar, were about five and twenty men, with their backs turned toward the Temple of the Lord" (or the Holy of Holies holding the Ark of the Covenant, the type of the perfect man, placed in the west, typical of the destiny of the race, toward which the worshipper was supposed to face while at prayer). These men had turned their backs upon this ideal, and were worshipping the sun towards the east gate, or the sun of the intellect, the lower mind. In other words they were materialists.

"Oh Son of Man, is it a light thing that they commit these abominations? They have filled the land with violence" (going against nature) "and have turned again to provoke Me to anger" (or to force Me to act as though I was angry). "They have put the branch in their nose." The ancients often used a forked stick to hook in the ring in the nose of a captive to lead him; hence the expression, they have put the branch, or the hooked stick to their own nose; they have enslaved themselves, they have brought upon themselves the effect of their own actions. The Kaballah says, "When it is written 'the anger of Tetragammaton will be kindled,' 'My wrath is kindled,' etc., it is understood to refer to Microprosopus" (or the god in the heart of man).

In this case it is Lord Jehovah showing this vision, not God Almighty, but the Great Lord in charge of physical conditions. The Lord Jehovah calls for the Destroying Angels, and they come from the way of the north, the way of the physical, each with a destroying weapon in his hand. Through the physical, or the personality, will destruction come. He then sent a scribe ahead of these destroyers to put a mark upon the forehead of all who sigh and cry over the abominations done in the land, all who have the higher ideal, who have developed the higher mind; and the command goes forth to utterly destroy all who have not this mark upon the forehead. To put it in other words, all who fail to develop the higher mind, and the higher ideals, will bring destruction upon themselves, as the cart follows the horse. It is but the natural effect of the misused energy. The destructive angels but symbolize the working out of natural law. "And it came to pass that I fell upon my face and cried, and said 'Oh, Lord Jehovah' (or Lord of Justice), 'wilt Thou destroy all of the residue of Israel in pouring out thy judgment upon the people?' And He said, 'The iniquity of the House of Israel is exceeding great, and the land is full of blood' (of innocent animals as well as people) 'and the city' (world) 'is full of perverse judgment.' (That has a distinctly modern sound, and might have been written yesterday.) 'For they say Jehovah hath forsaken the land, that Jehovah seeth not. I will bring their way upon their heads.' (Now note it is *their* way that is to be brought upon their heads.) 'As they sow so shall they also reap.' " Yet reading such passages as this, Christians of today deny the law of cause and effect, or Karma.

And the man with the inkhorn reported what he had done; that he had marked the ones to be saved, had noted the development of the higher mind. And the physical destroyers went forth to destroy—note that they are physical destroyers and can destroy only the physical. By a natural law by the misuse of the great creative force of the universe that is constantly poured out upon man to be by him passed on to others in blessing, in unselfish service, the selfish one consumes himself, and his physical body pays the penalty before the time it should have lived.

Occultism explains the way this acts, and the new chance given the person by a reincarnation in a new body in which he may redeem his past; but the time will come when the stubbornly perverse will be left behind, they will fall asleep not to waken for millions of years hence, when the planet again reaches the vibration to which they respond. This law is demonstrated in the west, or in any new country, on the Physical Plane. When the western ranchman turns water upon the cactus land, very often a very fine quality of hay will appear, grass that has never been seen in that locality in historic times. When the soil is plowed the first time, if the land is neglected the next year frequently the most luxuriant goldenrod appears. When the proper conditions are provided the seed that is in the earth germinates, and so it is with these egos; they will lie unconscious until the planet comes into their vibration again, or until nature forces transport them to some other planet where they find conditions favorable to their manifestation. This is as near destruction as humanity can ever get, and this is purely the result of their own actions, the direct effect of the causes that they have set in motion, that have lowered their vibrations until they can not respond to the higher rates of speed. There is no suffering in this state, simply unconsciousness, so the length of time causes no inconvenience to the ego.

High vibrations shatter the vehicles of one who is sensual, or selfish, so that when the whole planet vibrates at such a rate all such vehicles will simply disintegrate, leaving only the permanent atoms. This is probably the Day of Judgment spoken of in the Bible, and this also is the event referred to in this vision of Ezekiel. The six men with weapons mean the experiences of the six races which will purge and purify, or kill and disintegrate the bodies.

In Chapter x he continues: "I looked, and, behold, in the firmament, over the head of the cherubim there appeared above them, as it were, a sapphire stone, as the appearance of the likeness of a throne," evidently a symbol of the Christ, the Bodhisattva; and he tells the man clothed in white linen, significant of purity, to go between the wheels of the cherubim (the rounds of humanity), and take coals of fire and scatter them over the city; that is, scatter the fire of spirituality generated by humans, over the people. The cherubim are symbolic of the four rounds of humanity. The great wheels have wheels within wheels; the rounds have races within, and the races have sub-races; so here are wheels within wheels. The wheels are full of eyes, the eyes of humanity, and the cherubim have four faces. As the Hebrew made of man a quaternary, so these faces are: cherubim or the stage of innocence; second, man or mind, maturity, realization; third, lion, or strength, courage, development of the higher mind or soul; and fourth, eagle, or spiritual aspiration. "And the spirit of the Lord rested upon the cherubim, and they went and stood by the east gate of the Lord's house." Humanity stands at the gate of intellect, while the glory of the Lord rests upon them, waiting to enter the Temple of the Living God. And the cherubim traveled always straight ahead, the tide of evolution is ever onward ever upward, we are told.

You remember the five and twenty men we found worshipping the sun in the east, with their backs toward the west where sat the Holy Place containing the Ark of the Covenant, with their faces toward the east; they were worshipping the intellect. Ezekiel is told to prophesy against them, and he tells them that because of their iniquity the streets of the city, or the planet, will be strewn with the slain, "whom ye have laid in the midst of it"; their materialistic teachings have caused this lack of spiritual development, they teach the people that the time is not yet near to build houses (purified vehicles). This teaching has caused a great many to be rendered unfit for further progress, and they must be left behind as the wave of evolution rolls on. They are flesh, or physical, and this city, or planet, is the caldron. But ye (who are left behind) shall be brought forth out of it," he says; that is, in due time you will be brought to some place where you can finish your evolution.

"Ye have feared the sword" (revealed truth, the law), "the sword will I bring upon you," saith the Lord Jehovah. The law of cause and effect will bring upon them the things that they merit, and they will learn the truth. "And the word of the Lord came unto me saying, Son of man, thy brethren, the men of thy redemption, thy kindred, and all of the house of Israel, all of them, are they to whom the inhabitants of Jerusalem" (the Jews) "have said, get you far from the Lord, for unto us is given this land for a possession" (we are the chosen people).

"Therefore thus saith the Lord Jehovah: Whereas I have removed them" (the Israelites, the Aryan race proper) "far off among the nations, and whereas I have scattered them among the countries, yet will I be to them a sanctuary, for a little while in the countries where they are to come." That is, Lord Jehovah will be their sanctuary or their protection and guide, for awhile in the countries where they are to come, because they will be upon the purely Physical Plane. "Therefore thus saith the Lord Jehovah, I will gather you from the peoples, and will assemble you out of the countries where you have been scattered, and I will give you the land of Israel." Remember that we learned that the land of Israel was the extended consciousness given Jacob by his struggle with the angel (his higher self) and becoming conqueror with God, or conqueror over matter, the Christ consciousness. When he had attained this consciousness and had conquered the lower nature, as symbolized by the withered thigh, then, and not till then, did he become Israel, and enter into his inheritance. ("I will bring thee again to this land.")

So the prophesy goes on, "And I will give you one heart" (they shall enter the universal Christ vibration), "I will put a new spirit within them" (the Spirit of Christ) "and I will take away the stony heart out of their flesh, and give them a heart of flesh" (the Christ Spirit is one of compassion), "that they may walk in my statutes, and keep my ordinances to do them, and I will be their God, and they shall be My people" (they shall recognize the law of cause and effect as an active agency in the land); "but as for those whose heart walketh after the heart of their detestable things and their abominations, I will bring their way upon their own heads." Is not that a clear statement of Karma? Their way upon their own heads. They are not punished by an angry God, but by the natural effects of their own actions.

In Chapter XII it says: "The word of the Lord also came unto me saying, Son of man, thou dwellest in the midst of a rebellious house" (he was a Jew). "That have eyes to see and see not, and ears to hear and hear not, for they are a rebellious house." "Therefore, thou son of man, prepare thee thy stuff for removing, and remove by day in their sight. It may be that they will consider though they are a rebellious people." He was, in other words, to go out from them, or seek a higher plane of consciousness openly, make no secret that these things are possible, and telling them why it is desirable, so that they may be led to think. "Dig thou through the wall in their sight." (Wall is a symbol of the limitation set by the consciousness of the race.) They came to this stage of evolution through the gates of the physical (the north), the spiritual (the south), and the intellectual (the east). The gates were to enter by, but evidently this temple is not an earthly one, for the gates are not to go out by; he is to dig out through the walls to take his things out. He must transcend the evolution of the rest, taking his things or his consciousness through the wall he should do so openly or in sight of the rest, "but cover thy face that thou see not the land, for I have set thee as a sign for the house of Israel."

He was to make every endeavor to attain the higher consciousness, be perfectly frank about the advantages of such a course, but he would, after passing through the wall of the natural evolution of the race, find himself blind upon the higher plane to which he attained, for a time, but he was being pushed in his development for an example to the race. In the morning, he says (after he had attained) the Lord asked him if Israel had asked him "What doest thou?" And because of their indifference to the example set, because of their stiff-neckedness, they shall stay upon the Physical Plane and reap the ripe Karma that is waiting for them.

Here is enunciated one of the great occult laws, the law of Karma, or of action and reaction, cause and effect; for Karma is simply the result of causes that we have ourselves at sometime set in motion. Karmic vibrations, like all vibrations, travel in circles, reacting on the plane below the one on which they are sent forth. Physical Karma is often paid by the death of the body, astral or emotional Karma reacts on the Physical Plane, and mental Karma on the Emotional Plane. Suppose a man sends out a strong malignant vibration or thought form to some one. The nature of that thought form is to find the party toward whom it is directed and work its will upon him, then return to the sender. If the sender in the meantime gets a realization of his iniquity and repents, and enters into a vibration of intense aspiration for love, purity, and holiness, then the vibration of malignity will return to the place where it left him, because of the law; but also because of the law when it gets to where he should be according to that vibration, it will not be able to find him because he will be vibrating upon the planes above it, and it will pass under his feet, while the vibrations of love that he throws out will do much to neutralize it. So Ezekiel, here is trying to get the people to understand this law, and encourage them to rise above the limitations of the race and escape some of their race Karma, but as they refuse to accept the lesson, they must meet the effect of their past actions upon the Physical Plane, and when at last their prince does reach Babylon (the gate of God's House), he will be blind and unable to see the glories about him. The people shall be scattered among all nations (they shall be born many, many times among all nations) before they work out this load of Karma in the slow, natural evolutionary way.

Then he sees the Spirit of the Lord withdraw from the old Temple, with its north gate blocked by jealousy and sensuality, and its south, or spiritual gate defiled by the worship of the intellect and material things; and the Spirit rests upon the symbol of humanity. (No longer will the Spirit be confined to the external temple, but the heart of man will be its tabernacle.) This symbol, the cherubim and the wheels, resting upon the hills in the east, the elevations of intellectuality, or as Occultists would say, the higher mind. To make it plainer, the Spirit of God rested upon humanity as they rested upon the higher Mental Plane which is attained by a union of mind with spiritual aspiration; this is the plane that gives to man true wisdom.

In Chapter XLII we find Ezekiel describing another temple; now note the measurements, five hundred reeds by five hundred reeds, that is, the wall is the limitation set by the development of the race, which is the fifth race. This temple wall marks the limit of the consciousness of the fifth race after it has been trained by the experience of the ages. Humanity, hereafter to be the Temple of the Living God.

He brought me to the gate, even to the gate that looketh to

the east. You remember we left the cherubim, or humanity resting upon the hills of the east, resting in the higher mind with God's Glory overshadowing them. So now the glory of the God of Israel (fifth root race) came by way of the east, or the intellect. The fifth root race is not to worship in blind superstition, nor from compulsion, but from intellectual comprehension.

And "His voice was like the sound of many waters." The truth will flow from many sources. "And the earth shined in His Glory." God's true wisdom will irradiate everything. "And the glory of the Lord entered into the temple" (of the race as a race, through the door of the intellect, Chapters 43-4), "and the glory of the Lord came into the house" (man) "by way of the east gate.

"And the Spirit of the Lord took me into the inner court" (the heart), "and behold, the glory of the Lord filled the house." And he said unto me, "Son of man, this is the place of my throne, and the place of the soles of my feet, where I will dwell in the midst of the house of Israel forever." Let them put away the dead bodies of their kings (their personalities that have been ruling them), and I will dwell in the midst of them forever, if they will be ashamed of the things they have done and will keep the good law (the law of evolution). Then follows a very elaborate description of the temple furnishings, its laws, etc., for which we have not the space at this time.

Chapter XLVII says: "And he brought me back to the door of the house" (this Temple of the Living God, the God-man), "and behold, waters issued forth from beneath the threshold of the house eastward." Waters of wisdom coming from the south, or spiritual side of the altar (heart) rushed out of the gate of the intellect. Intellect refined by Spirit gave out a flood of wisdom. "And he measured one thousand cubits and made me pass through the waters, and them came up to the ankles." (He entered the stream of wisdom and took the first Initiation.)

Then he measured one thousand cubits again, and caused him to pass through again, and this time the waters of wisdom came up to the knees. (He took a second Initiation, or was shown what a second Initiation meant).

"And again he measured one thousand cubits and caused me

to pass through, and the waters came to the loins." (Symbolic of the third Initiation.)

"Afterward he measured a thousand and behold a river to swim in." (The entire nature is submerged in the waters of wisdom, the fourth great Initiation.) Then he shows him how this river of wisdom flowing from the Temple of the Living God, or the regenerated heart of man, will fructify and sweeten the land and sea of humanity. How great trees, or great teachers, will grow on the banks; how the great restless sea of humanity in evolution will be strengthened and sweetened in their consciousness and healed of their iniquities.

He is then shown that the inheritance of Israel is to be divided equally between the tribes, or each man has an equal chance to obtain this extended consciousness. Each man to have his portion, each man to enter into his inheritance of this higher consciousness, and the whole to be offered as an oblation to the Great Supreme One. You will notice that the oblation is to measure twenty-five thousand reeds, or units (miles), by twenty-five thousand (the circumference of the earth is twenty-five thousand miles, so the whole planet is meant), and the new city measures forty-five hundred reeds by forty-five hundred reeds, or the fourth round and the fifth root race; so here is set the limits of the consciousness to be attained by the fifth root race now in the fourth round. In this city (the world) He sees all men dwelling in peace and enjoying to the full their inheritance of Divine Consciousness, all devoted to the Supreme One, and the name of the city shall be "God is There," for each man will have found the God within his own heart, and will understand the meaning of the words, "The cord of the inheritance of Jacob," and "the God of Israel." Each man a "cephas," or "stone," carved without hands, fit to be placed in the walls of the Temple of the Living God, and he shall "go no more out" as John says. "Behold the Temple of God is with man, the first things are passed away, and he that sitteth upon the throne saith, 'Behold, I will make all things new.'"

CHAPTER XIII.

JEHOVAH COMMANDED NO BLOODY SACRIFICES.

Let us glance for a moment at one phase of misconception caused by the literal reading of what was probably meant in the beginning to be taken symbolically only, namely: the command to slay innocent animals in religious service.

The Kabbalah says (page 91, paragraph 7): "When inferior man descendeth (into this world) like unto the Supernal form there are found two spirits. . . . With respect unto the right side he hath the holy intelligences. With respect to the left side, the animal soul." Here we may assume was the animal that God expected to be sacrificed upon the altar.

Page 316, paragraph 565: "Hence it is written Gen. VIII. 21. And JHVH smelled a sweet savor". It is not written, He smells the odor of sacrifice. What is sweet save rest? Assuredly the Spirit at rest is the mitigation of the Lords of judgment. When therefore it is said that JHVH smelled the odor of rest, most certainly the odor of sacrificed victims is not meant, but the odor of those mitigations of severity which are referred to the nose of Microprosopus (man)."

"From the nose of Microprosopus proceedeth from one nostril smoke and fire, and from the other peace and beneficent Spirits."

We know from history that the Jews actually slaughtered animals in their religious services, using blood as a symbol of the sacrifice man should make of his animal nature, but we do not know when it was first introduced. That it was permitted to go on so long indicates that there must have been some good purpose in it, but when one studies deeply into the spirit of the inner teaching of the Grand Old Book one seems to be justified in assuming that those services must have crept in after the priests had forgotten the real Mystery teaching. This seems especially probable when we consider that the race has outgrown those ideas and have really come to abhor that form of worship while studying the very book that seems to teach it. To be sure we are taught in Christian churches that Jesus died once for all, but the Jew does not believe that, yet he too in this country usually worships without the bloody sacrifice.

We find the first mention of animal sacrifice in Gen. IV, 2. Abel (Spirit) was a shepherd (teacher) and Cain (possessor) was a tiller of the ground (he cultivated his physical propensities). That is, humanity had come into incarnation with dual natures, therefore Cain and Abel are spoken of as twins. The animal instincts are so strong that they kill out the "Abel," or Spirit, when it remonstrates. The Spirit would have placed its whole animal nature on the altar, and have offered up the first fruits of its teaching to others willingly, because that was its nature; but Cain, the physical, would offer up anything else rather than its animal nature. Because he chooses the life of animal gratification rather than the true life, Lord Jehovah tells him he has brought the curse upon him; that is, he will have to suffer from the law of cause and effect, and will be a wanderer on the Physical Plane until he learns to offer the "reasonable service," the crucifixion of the lower self.

Read literally, Leviticus I seems to make Jehovah the author of animal sacrifice; but read symbolically another story is told. And may it not be that when first given out the true meaning was understood, but in the course of ages, because of the laxity of the priesthood, this was lost, and gradually the lower conception became established?

This seems to be a reasonable view if we take the testimony of Scripture itself. In Jeremiah VII, 21, we read: "Thus saith Jehovah of Hosts: For I spake not unto your fathers nor commanded them in the day I brought them out of the land of Egypt" (ignorance and sin) "concerning burnt offerings and sacrifices." This is certainly a plain statement, and with just the same authority that we supposed Leviticus to have.

23. "But this thing I commanded them saying, hearken unto My voice, and I will be your God, and ye shall be My people; and walk in all the way I command you that it may be well with you. 24. But they hearkened not nor inclined their ears, but walked in their own councils, and the stubbornness of their evil heart and

went backward and not forward." (They offered up poor innocent animals instead of their own animal nature.) 25. Since the day that your fathers came forth out of the land of Egypt I have sent all My servants and prophets daily, rising up early and sending them" (symbolic), "yet they hearken not unto Me, nor incline their ear, but make their neck stiff; they did worse than their fathers. . . . . . 30. For the children of Judah have done that which was evil in My sight, saith Jehovah; they have set their abominations in the house that is called by my name to defile it." (Altars upon which poor animals were offered.)

In Psalms LI, 16, we are told, "For thou delightest *not in sacrifice; else would I give it.*" (So there must have been a time when this was understood. David seems to have understood it.)

"Thou hast *no pleasure* in burnt offerings."

17. "The sacrifices of God are a broken Spirit,
A broken and a contrite heart, O God, Thou wilt not despise."

In Hosea VI: "For I desire goodness and not sacrifice; and the knowledge of God is more than burnt offerings."

7. "But they like Adam have transgressed the covenant, they have dealt treacherously against Me "

8. "Gilead is a city of them that work iniquity; it is stained with blood" (of the poor animals slaughtered).

9. "And as troops of robbers wait for a man so the company of *priests murder in the way to Shechem.*" (Shechem was a very fertile valley where many herds grazed, watering at Jacob's well.)

10. "In the house of Israel I have seen a *horrible thing.*" (The blood of animals used as a religious rite.)

In Hosea VIII, 13: "As for the sacrifices of mine offerings, they sacrifice flesh and eat it; but Jehovah *accepteth them not; now* will He *remember* their *iniquity.*"

In the answer of the scribe to Jesus as given us by Mark XII, 32, "And the scribe said unto Him, Of a truth Teacher, Thou hast well said that He is One; and there is none other but He. 33. And to love Him with all the heart, and with all the understanding, and with all the strength, and to love his neighbor as himself, is much more than all whole burnt offering and sacrifice. 34. And when Jesus saw that he answered Him *discreetly,* He said unto him, 'Thou art not far from the kingdom of God.'"

In I Sam. xv, 22, we are told that "To obey is better than sacrifice."

Prov. xxi, 3: "To do righteousness and justice is more acceptable to Jehovah than sacrifice."

Amos v, 21-22: "I hate, I despise your feasts, and I will take no delight in your solemn assemblies. 23. Yea, though ye offer Me your burnt offerings and your meal offerings, I will not accept them, neither will I regard the peace offerings of your fat beasts. . . . . . 24. But let justice roll down as waters, and righteousness as a mighty stream."

Isaiah i, 11: "What unto Me is the multitude of your sacrifices? said Jehovah: I have had enough of the burnt offerings of rams, and the fat of fed beasts. I delight not in the blood of bullocks or of lambs or of he goats."

12. "When ye come to appear before Me, who hath required this at your hand? . . . . . 13. "Bring no more vain oblations, incense is an abomination to Me." 14. "Your new moons and your appointed feasts My soul hateth; they are a trouble unto Me. I am weary of bearing them. 15. When ye spread forth your hands, I will hide Mine eyes from you; Yea, when ye make many prayers I will not hear, your hands are full of blood."

16. "Wash you make you clean; put away the evil in your doings from before Mine eyes, cease to do evil. 17. Learn to do well, seek justice, relieve the oppressed, judge the fatherless, plead for the widow."

18. "Come now let us reason together, saith Jehovah; Though your sins be as scarlet they shall be white as snow." 19. "If ye be willing and obedient ye shall eat of the good of the land."

Jeremiah vi, 20: Your burnt offerings are not acceptable nor your sacrifices pleasing unto Me."

Malachi ii, 4: "My covenant may be with Levi, saith Jehovah. 5. My covenant was with him of life and peace" (not death and destruction).

6. "The law of truth was in his mouth, and unrighteousness was not found in his lips, he walked with me in peace and uprightness and turned many away from iniquity."

7. "For the priests' lips should keep knowledge" (they should not have lost the knowledge of the Mysteries of their religion so

JEHOVAH COMMANDED NO BLOODY SACRIFICES

that such abuses could have crept in), "and they should seek law at his mouth; for he is the messenger of Jehovah of Hosts."

8. "But ye turned aside out of the way; ye have caused many to stumble in the law; ye have corrupted the covenant of Levi, saith Jehovah of Hosts."

Malachi III, 7: "From the days of your fathers ye have turned aside from mine ordinances and have not kept them" (but they kept up their burnt offerings).

8. "Wherein have we robbed thee? The answer is in tithes and heave offerings" (the heaving hearts of the men).

Ezekiel XXXIII, 25: "Wherefore say unto them, Thus saith the Lord Jehovah, Ye eat with the blood, and lift up your eyes unto your idols, and shed blood, and shall ye possess the land?"

29. "Then shall they know that I am Jehovah when I have made the land a desolation and an astonishment because of all their abominations which they have committed."

Ezekiel XXXVI, 17: "Son of man, when the house of Israel dwelt in their own land, they defiled it by their way, and by their doings; their way before me was as the uncleanness of a woman in her impurity."

18. "Wherefore I poured out my wrath upon them" (that is, let them learn the law of cause and effect), "for the blood which they had poured out upon the land because they had defiled it with their idols" (or their worship).

And what is the promise to Israel after the suffering she has brought upon herself has purified her?

Ezekiel XXXVI, 25: "I will sprinkle you with clean waters" (sign of purification) "and ye shall be clean; from all of your filthiness and from all your idols will I cleanse you."

26. "A new heart also will I give you, and a new spirit will I put within you; and I will take away the stony heart out of your flesh" (the heart that could kill poor innocent animals), "and I will give you a heart of flesh." 27. "And I will put my spirit within you." . . . . . 29. "And I will save you from all your uncleanness."

Does it not seem probable that the world has had a gross misconception of the teachings of our Sacred Book?

In Psalms XL, 6, we read: "Sacrifice and offerings thou hast no delight in, my ears hast thou opened. Burnt offering and sin offering hast thou not required. Then I said, Lo I come to do thy will, O my God. Yea, thy law is written on my heart."

The only account we have of Jesus showing anger is in John II, 14, when He drove the money changers from the Temple (the people who sold animals and birds for sacrifice). His words were: "It is written my house shall be called a house of prayer, but ye have made it a den of robbers." Surely these are strong words in support of our argument.

Oh, friends, let us study our Sacred Book and develop the intuition that it is designed to develop, and show to suffering humanity the God of Love that the inner record reveals. It is high time that the white light of truth be thrown upon these books so that man may no more hide behind Sacred Writ for authority to kill either his brother man or his younger brothers the animals.

CHAPTER XIV.

LIGHT THROWN UPON OBSCURE PASSAGES.

It may be well to show in a few words how much light is shed upon obscure passages in Scripture by this symbolic reading, light that will prevent much skepticism when it becomes generally diffused.

Take, for instance, the statement that Joshua commanded the sun to stand still, and she stood. Now every schoolboy knows that it is simply an impossibility as read literally. In the light of this understanding all becomes luminous.

The symbol of the Lord Jehovah is the moon. The symbol of the Christ is the sun. The word "Joshua" means "Jesus," which means the help of Jehovah. As we study the life of Jesus we see that His especial work (as it is of many other Masters also) is to to assist humanity to conquer their desire natures, and build up purified vehicles in which the Christ child can be born. He leads them in their great struggle between Spirit and matter.

Now consider the allegory. Joshua (Jesus) is leading His people to battle on the spiritual hillsides. He says to Lord Jehovah, "Moon, stand thou still over the valley of Aijalon" (field of the animals, man on the animal plane), "and Sun" (Christ) "over Gideon" (Mount of Initiation) "only give me double time, for this is a fierce struggle." And double time was given Him, but more were conquered (slain) by the hailstones than by the sword. More were conquered by hard natural experiences than by the teachings of the truth.

To this day Jesus still stands on these same hillsides, helping us fight our battle against the flesh, and the Lord Jehovah still guards and guides the animal man, and still the great Christ stands on the Mount of Initiation ready to glorify those who win in the struggle and reach up to Him clean hands and a contrite heart, wholly consecrated to do the will of the Father. Thus, all through the ages have the Initiations been going on as fast as a man could be found who was worthy; thus are they still going on, and so will they ever be given so long as a man lives who will be helped by their assistance.

Take the story of Jonah that has given so much trouble to teachers because of the evident absurdities of the literal reading of the tale. Everyone today knows that a whale cannot swallow a man, and every Biblical student knows that the word translated whale should have been translated big fish.

Now we find that one of the local usages of the region in which the episode of Jonah is placed is to call the caves washed out by the waves along the coast by the same name that was used in the account to describe the one that swallowed Jonah. One who has traveled extensively along that coast says that these caves often have plenty of dry land in the back part, but frequently the mouths are covered by the incoming tide or by a storm that blows landward. By looking it up you will find that Jesus uses the same word when he speaks of the incident; that is, the same Greek word that means fish. He tells us that these caves often are inhabited during storms by those who get caught there, just as Jonah was, and are obliged to stay there till the storm dies down and allows them to escape.

Now read Jonah and see if the story is not quite probable and natural.

Jonah II, 2: "Out of the belly of Sheol" (the pit) "cried I, 3, For thou didst cast me into the depth, in the heart of the seas And the flood was round about me;
And thy waves and thy billows passed over me . . . . .
The seaweeds were wrapped about my head.
I went to the bottoms of the mountains;
The earth with its bars closed over me forever" (not a fish with whalebones).

"Yet hast thou brought up my life from the pit, O Jehovah my God."

So much for the literal historic basis for the story. Not at all improbable.

Now let us look at it as an allegory of Initiation.

First, Jonah hears the call of God to go and preach to Ninevah, but he was not ready to answer to that call: "Lo, I come to do thy will, O God," so he sails out on the sea of desire. When he tries that, he finds his rebellion to God sets up a great commotion among the very elements (storm). His companions, when they find he is acting in defiance to God, throw him overboard. They are gratifying desire, but with no especial rebellion to God in their hearts; they are simply following the dictates of their animal soul, with no other thought than the pleasure of the gratification of the desire. When they see a case of real defiance against God they are afraid, and they cast him overboard.

He is buried in the sea of desire till he sinks to the depths; then, when he cries to God in real penitence, he finds himself in the cave of Initiation, Jesus speaks of his being three days and three nights in the cave, evidently thinking of His own Initiation so soon to be accomplished.

Jonah is given the Initiation and comes forth ready to do God's will, and he does it. But we are told that after every Initiation we are born upon the higher plane a babe, so we are shown the baby side of Jonah He preaches all right, and then pouts because God does not kill the people even though they did repent. He pouts because the gourd dies, and he pouts when the Lord remonstrates with him. He is a babe just born into the kingdom.

"Jacob have I loved, Esau have I hated," says the Scripture; and we wonder how that can be. It is cleared up when we read in the "Kabbalah" that Edom and Esau stand in Scripture for unbalanced forces in man, while Jacob stands for the balanced nature. Jacob conquered his lower nature and let his angel, or his higher self, conquer.

The falling of the walls of Jericho is also explained very simply when we understand the symbolism. Walls are symbolic of the consciousness of a people. Jericho was a stronghold of the Atlantean Moon worship. Joshua commanded his people to march around the walls each day of the week, blowing upon the ram's horn, or exalting the Lamb that was slain from the beginning of the world, while following the Ark, the symbol of the Perfect Man.

The Ark is carried by the priests, while the mass of the people follow two thousand cubits behind, or two great races behind. Thus they live the Godly life six days in the week, doing it seven times as strong on Sabbath, and the walls of the city fall, or the consciousness of the people is conquered. They see the significance of the life really lived, and necromancy is conquered. Rahab the harlot, a school of broad wisdom, is saved and protected because of the crimson cord of love she threw out of the window, or on the upper planes. She is seeking truth from any source, and love is the basis of her teachings.

LIST OF SYMBOLIC AND OBSOLETE MEANINGS OF WORDS.

Abagail, father of joy (masc.).
Abominations, going against God's will.
Abijah, same as Adonis, my father is Jehovah.
Adultery, studying with many schools.
AI, heap of ruins, symbol of the fourth root race.
Ahinoam, brother of delight (masc.).
Amen, in the light of two countenances, that of God above and that of the God within.
Amraphel, keeper of the Gods.
Amonite, mountaineer (spiritual).
Angel, messenger, or the higher self.
Animals, ass, bear, mule, lion and others mean the animal nature.
Aaron, lofty teacher.
Arm, power.
Armor, equipment of character.
Armor bearer, the heart.
Arioch, venerable, King of Ellasar, Oak.
Arrows, words, teachings; *Shafts* have the same meaning.
Aryeh, Hebrew for Lion; *Judah,* the lion's whelp.
Aryan (aryeh), fifth root race.
Asses, common people, particularly the common people of the fourth root race.

Babes, inexperienced, those who had taken the first great Initiation.
Babylon, gate of God, or gate of Initiation, symbolically.
Baptism, the second great Initiation.
Bath-Sheba, well of the oath or daughter of the oath, or well of seven.
Beasts, animal propensities, or cruel people, people on the animal plane.
Bera, son of evil, king of Sodom.
Bethel, Temple of God (Ye are the Temples of the Living God).
Beth-peor, house of the cleft.
Bethuel, dweller in God.
Bethlehem, house of bread (spiritual bread).
Birth, first Initiation.
Birsha, son of godlessness, King of Gomorah.
Body, an organized living system, as a church or community.
Bow, strength.
Blood, natural descent. Symbolically life, "The blood is the life thereof."
Brass, judgment.
Bread, food on any plane.

AN ESOTERIC READING OF BIBLICAL SYMBOLISM

Briars, or thorns, perverse or injurious persons or things.
Bride, the manifestation of the H, the creative love wisdom manifestation of God on the four lower planes.
Brimstone and fire, great suffering on both Physical and Astral planes, sometimes destruction.
Bulls, furious strong foes, or simply strong animal nature.

Caanan, low-lying land.
Calf, physical creative energy.
Cedars, great men.
Cedars of Lebanon, kings and great men. Top branches, princes and nobility. Men of learning, godliness, and strength of character.
Chaff, worthless persons.
Chedorloamer, servant of justice.
Chain, bondage, affliction.
Christ, Messiah, the anointed one, also a degree of consciousness of the Intuitional Plane.
Circumcision, purification.
Cities, races, or the extent of consciousness of a people, especially the wall of a city, which defines the extent of the consciousness of the people.
Clean teeth, hunger.
Consort, associate with.
Copper, judgment.
Cornerstone, the basic truth of a system.
Cross, the fleshly body or a burden of any kind.
Crown (kether), an honor, or the streams of God's power that play upon man.
Cup, according to the contents, either blessings or otherwise.

Damnation, condemnation.
Darkness, inharmony, sin, ignorance.
Darkness of the sun, and moon, losing sight of Christ and Lord Jehovah.
Daughter, city, community or class in Mystery work.
David, beloved.
Day, period of time, light order, harmony.
Death, separation from God, worldliness, buried in the physical.
Dew, divine influence.
Dogs, those outside of the order spoken of, sometimes wicked people.
Door (open), opportunity.
Drunken, spiritual ecstasy.
Dust, mental matter.
Dust and ashes, human disappointment.

Eagle, great leader, high aspirations.
East, intellectuality.
Earthquake, political or spiritual revolutions.
Egypt, Physical Plane, black land, land of Cush.
Elizabeth, the oath of God.
Ephraim, double fruitfulness.

LIST OF SYMBOLIC AND OBSOLETE MEANINGS OF WORDS

Esau, unbalanced force; sometimes the fourth and a half root race. A mongrel race neither the one nor the other.
Eye, moral or spiritual discernment.
Eye of God. God has but one eye, because with Him all things are right He has no left side, symbolically.

Face or countenance of God, the great face.
Face (little face), God in the heart of man.
Famine, symbol of lack of truth.
Fig tree, symbol of creative force.
Fire and brimstone, spiritual and physical forces.
Fire, spirituality.
Flood, overwhelmed.
Fornication, studying foreign systems of thought.
Four, complete physical, foundation.
Fox, quiet unassuming teacher.
Fruit, results of actions.
Furnace, severe testing afflictions.

Galilee, circuit.
Garments, sometimes bodies, sometimes arguments.
Gates, seats of power
Gates of death, peril of life.
Girdle, tightened, preparation for energetic action. Transferred to another symbol of transferred authority.
Girgashites, dwellers on clay.
Goats, perverse people of the Aryan stock
God's face, mercy. *Face of the Son,* wisdom and love. *Face of the earth,* understanding.
God swore, means that God lifted His hand with the sign of power.
Gold, God's wisdom, and righteousness.
Gommorah, submerged.
Grass, weak humanity.
Growth, increase in righteousness.

H. Hevah, translated Eve, Second Person of the Trinity. No matter upon which plane it manifests.
Hail, hardened material forces.
Hagar, bondage of ignorance.
Hair, streams of God's creative energy.
Hand, power; *right hand,* might, place of honor.
Harlot, school of broad wisdom.
Harvest, season of privilege.
Heaven, state of consciousness of the Intuitional Plane. Kingdom of Heaven means sometimes the Great White Lodge.
Hebrews, those who have crossed over (into the new race).
Heifer, physical creative activity.
Hell, from root meaning to hide, hidden unseen, symbolically depths of ruin or despair.

AN ESOTERIC READING OF BIBLICAL SYMBOLISM

Hittites, low people.
Herod, symbol of material power.
Horn, power, wisdom.
Horse, conquering might.
House, body.
Hunger, intense desire.

IHVH, Jehovah, the Trinity of manifestations of the Supreme; first, on the higher planes; second, Lord Jehovah, the Great One who looks after the material welfare of the race on the Physical Plane; third, Jehovah of Hosts, the God in the heart of every man.
Incense, prayer. *Burnt incense,* Spiritual prayer.
Ish, man; *Ishah,* woman or the completion of man, or his body.
Israel, Aryan race, not the Jews. Also the father of the race.
Israel, the prince that prevails with God.
Iron, oppression

Jacob, supplanter, Aryan race, as well as the founder of the race.
Jebusites, threshers.
John, gift of Jehovah, teacher.
Joseph, increased consciousness.
Jerusalem, peace
Jesus, help of Jehovah.
Judah, praised, celebrated, Jews, the sister of Israel.
Jehovah, see IHVH. Lord Jehovah is used in the same sense as the Hindoo Vaivasvatta.

Kadmonites, children of the east, or intellectuality.
Keys, authority, knowledge.
Kenites, smiths.
Kenizites, hunters.
Kine, animal nature, sometimes wealthy proud rulers.

Laban, White Brother.
Lamb, Christ, humility, gentleness.
Lambs, younger members of Mystery work; young Initiates.
Lamp or *torch,* illumination or illuminator, teacher; sometimes royal succession.
Lawyer, expounder of Mosaic Law.
Leaven, any diffusive influence.
Leaves, outward show.
Let, hinder or prevent.
Lewdness, wickedness of any kind; villainy.
Libertine, child of a freed slave.
Life, union of the soul with God.
Light, order, harmony with God's law, knowledge, purity.
Lion, strength, boldness; sometimes the animal nature, sometimes an astrological sign.
List, desire, will, like.
Locusts, multitudinous wasting enemies.
Loins girded, ready for action.

LIST OF SYMBOLIC AND OBSOLETE MEANINGS OF WORDS

Máia, mother Mary, (suggests Sanscrit, Maya, illusion).
Manassah, mental giants.
Manna, food from above.
Manu, father of a race, over lord of the Physical Plane.
Mansions, resting places.
Manger of stable, inmost recesses of man's heart; the inner place in his animal nature.
Marriage, union with God.
Meat, food of any kind.
Meat offerings consisted of only flour and oil.
Mess, dish of any kind of food.
Michael, like unto God.
Milk, weak food; elementary truths.
Mother, H, the love wisdom creative outflow of the higher planes, the manifestation of the Second Person of the Trinity.
Mountain, Mount of Initiation, or high spiritual elevation.
Myrtle, earth.

Nazareth, guarded one, a seat of Mystery work.
Naked, without possessions, or without bodies, without experience.
Nebo, Mount of Initiation in Mysteries of Nebo.
Night, darkness of mind, inharmony with God.
Numbers: 1, God; 2, positive and negative, symbol of the Second Person of the Trinity; 3, Trinity as a whole; 4, physical perfection, foundation; 5, symbol of harvest; 6, balanced Karma; 7, perfection, sacred number of completion; 8, double quaternary symbol of completion; 9, triune man, complete on the three planes; 10, man complete in his kingdom or aura.
666 Nero, Cæsar written in Hebrew characters.

Oaks, strong teachers.
Olive, regenerate man, or simply man.
Olive fields, communities of men; *wild olive,* unregenerate man.
Over against, east of.

Palm tree, fruitfulness of character; sometimes air.
Passover, the turning point in man's life, when he definitely turns to God, and sprinkles the life (blood) of the Christ upon the lintels of the doorposts of his heart.
Pestilence, purification.
Perizites, important people.
Pillar, support of a structure.
Pomegranate, fruitfulness.
Poison, falsehood, malignity.
Prevent, go before, precede.
Pharaoh, sometimes the great hierophant of Mystery work, sometimes the symbol of material power.
Prophecy, expounding.
Provoke, stimulate to action.

Rachel, God's productive pupil.
Rahab, broad freedom.

AN ESOTERIC READING OF BIBLICAL SYMBOLISM

Rain, divine influence, blessings, pure instruction.
Rainbow, covenant, universal covenant.
Ravening, greedy, rapacious.
Red, sometimes war, sometimes humanity.
Red Sea, properly rendered means sea of things.
Reins, emotions, affections.
Rephaim, giants.
River, wisdom, flood, invasion, or submersion. *Two rivers*, or plane of two rivers, means the Physical and Astral planes.
Rock, Master of Compassion. *Stone* means the same.
Rod, thyrsus, rod of Initiation into the Mysteries.

Sarah, free princess.
Sarai, my princess, bound.
Salt, purity, preservative, sound doctrines, good character.
Sea, people, Desire Plane, sometimes Mystery, depth.
Seal, security, perfection, exclusive claim.
Serpent, wisdom; *brazen serpent*, true wisdom; *black serpent*, black art; *fiery serpents*, lust, or improper use of creative wisdom.
Shadow, body or astral body, sometimes grief.
Silver, regeneration.
Seed, those of the faith.
Sheep, Aryan people. ''The sheep are my people.''
Shechinah, divine downpouring.
Shemeber, highflier.
Shepherds, teachers, leaders. *Shepherds at night*, teachers *on the Astral Planes*.
Shield, defense.
Shinar, land of two rivers.
Shinab, earthly splendor.
Silence, ruin.
Sodom, burning.
Sores, sins, also ulcers.
Stars, egos, sometimes rulers.
Stone, Master of Compassion.
Straight, narrow.
Straightly, strictly.
Straightness, scarcity of food.
Sword, truth.
Sun, Christ.

Tabernacle, body of the soul; sometimes Mystery work, sometimes place of worship.
Teeth, grinding, cruelty and greed; *clean teeth*, hunger.
Temple, the abode of God; man's heart.
Thousand, one great race; *1,000 cubits*, one great race; *hundred cubits*, one subrace.
Threshing, purifying.
Throne, peaceful government, lofty position, one of power.
Thunders, declaration of God's will.

LIST OF SYMBOLIC AND OBSOLETE MEANINGS OF WORDS

Tidal, Great Son King of nations.
Tongues, languages.
Towers, defenses.
Translate, remove.
Trees, teachers, men in authority; *green trees,* teachers of black art.
Turtle doves, IH Spirit.
Trow, think.

Vine, Christ; *branches,* the people who depend upon Him.
Vineyard, spiritual retreat or exercises of a spiritual nature; *fruit of the vine,* spiritual impulses.
Viper, dangerous foe.
Virgin, pure of either sex; *virgin matter,* matter that has been unproductive.

Walking with, being one with.
Wall, the extent of a people's consciousness.
Ware, aware.
Washing, purifying spiritually.
Water, wisdom.
Wax, grow, become.
Wealth, prosperity.
Well, symbol of deep wisdom.
Wheat, rich blessings, holy people.
White, purity, truth.
Wilderness, ignorance, adversity.
Willow, water.
Wind, spirit; sometimes symbolic of destructive forces.
Wine, spirituality. *Wine, corn and oil* abundance of spirituality, physical strength and wisdom. *Wine press, treading it,* judgments to develop spirituality.
Wings, protection, speed.
Winnowing, driving away the wicked, purifying.
Wolf, faithless pastor or teacher.
Woman, the completion of man.
Woman, the creative love wisdom outflow of the supreme in manifestation. Sometimes it is the vehicles of man, the bodies he wears; sometimes of a church; sometimes a Mystery lodge; sometimes a community or city.
Wrath, accomplished Karma.

Yoke, union, or restraint.
Young pigeon, VH, creative energy of lower planes.

Deacidified using the Bookkeeper process
Neutralizing agent Magnesium Oxide
Treatment Date May 2005

PreservationTechnologies

CPSIA information can be obtained
at www.ICGtesting.com
Printed in the USA
BVHW030911031122
650963BV00005B/134